All the Rage

POETS ON POETRY

David Lehman, General Editor
Donald Hall, Founding Editor

New titles

William Logan, *All the Rage*
Anne Stevenson, *Between the Iceberg and the Ship*
C. K. Williams, *Poetry and Consciousness*

Recently published

Allen Grossman, *The Long Schoolroom*
Jonathan Holden, *Guns and Boyhood in America*
Andrew Hudgins, *The Glass Anvil*
Josephine Jacobsen, *The Instant of Knowing*
Carol Muske, *Women and Poetry*
Charles Simic, *Orphan Factory*
William Stafford, *Crossing Unmarked Snow*
May Swenson, *Made with Words*

Also available are collections by

A. R. Ammons, Robert Bly, Philip Booth, Marianne Boruch,
Hayden Carruth, Fred Chappell, Amy Clampitt, Tom Clark,
Douglas Crase, Robert Creeley, Donald Davie, Peter Davison,
Tess Gallagher, Suzanne Gardinier, Thom Gunn, John Haines,
Donald Hall, Joy Harjo, Robert Hayden, Daniel Hoffman,
Weldon Kees, Galway Kinnell, Mary Kinzie, Kenneth Koch,
Richard Kostelanetz, Maxine Kumin, Martin Lammon (editor),
David Lehman, Philip Levine, John Logan, William Matthews,
William Meredith, Jane Miller, John Frederick Nims, Gregory Orr,
Alicia Ostriker, Marge Piercy, Anne Sexton, Charles Simic,
Louis Simpson, William Stafford, Richard Tillinghast,
Diane Wakoski, Alan Williamson, Charles Wright, and
James Wright

William Logan

All the Rage

Ann Arbor
THE UNIVERSITY OF MICHIGAN PRESS

2001   2000   1999   1998   4   3   2   1

A CIP catalog record for this book is available from the British Library.

Library of Congress Cataloging-in-Publication Data

Logan, William, 1950–
    All the rage / William Logan.
        p.   cm. — (Poets on poetry)
    ISBN 0-472-09631-1 (alk. paper). — ISBN 0-472-06631-5 (pbk. :
alk. paper)
    1. American poetry—20th century—History and criticism.
    2. English poetry—20th century—History and criticism.   I. Title.
II. Series.
PS323.5.L64   1998
811'.509—dc21   97-52823
                                                               CIP

for R. P. Blackmur and Randall Jarrell

Seems to me, then, this geniality you say you feel waked in you, is as water-power in a land without mills.

—THE CONFIDENCE MAN

Contents

Preface

This book contains all my apprentice criticism I care to see collected. I am grateful to the editors who first invited me to write about poetry, John Blades of the *Chicago Tribune* and Daryl Hine of *Poetry*. I was originally a reviewer of fiction, for which I had a reader's taste rather than a writer's intuition; but I remember the fresh anticipations brought by the arrival of each month's heavy, padded bags at my apartment on Provincetown harbor. I cannot pretend I felt a calling to criticism, though I believe it a duty partly moral (perhaps three-fifths pleasure and two-fifths moral). As Eliot wrote to Pound, "I am . . . expected . . . to write articles for the *Times* which are also of no use and furthermore are said to damage my brain. My dear Ezra, I don't want to write articles for the *Times* or for anything else, I don't want to write articles at all, I don't want to write, no sensible man does who wants to write verse." But there have been certain pleasures in pursuing a calling I believe is not my own.

I have condensed the longer, lankier reviews and often rewritten a sentence, changed a word, or restored an earlier reading. Where I have revised, I have attempted to improve the prose without altering the opinions. All the reviews were commissioned, but not all were printed. I have noted the date of original composition in the acknowledgments.

The Prejudice of Aesthetics

Aesthetics, like criticism, is an attempt to justify prejudice, not explain it. That a poet's aesthetics is normally drawn from his practice is no guarantee the principle or the practice will actually be sensible. In the worst case they will not even be congruent. With those poets least cursed with talent, however, it is a social good when their preaching does not conform to their practice, at least if one believes no procedure could be more damaging than the procedure of their poetry.

A whole generation of poets now maturing has been educated in brutal indifference to the technical complications of the art—rhyme, meter, the shape and support of stanzas, all those formal devices of music and metaphor that condition meaning. It isn't that most poets don't use these devices in piecemeal fashion; it's that the effects are often piecemeal as well. What for most poets passes as craft is sensibility or the presentation of subject. William Carlos Williams warned that "when a poet, in the broadest sense, begins to devote himself to the *subject matter* of his poems, *genre,* he has come to an end of his poetic means." In the quicksand of *Paterson,* his subject became the petty deity of form. The tyranny of material has reached an unforgivable state in our poetry. It is as if sculptors had been instructed that, their only concern being the provenance of the marble, the use of chisels was a moral offense.

I wish to examine the prejudices behind some contemporary statements on aesthetics (moving downward to include matters of form and craft that have a bearing on aesthetic belief or aesthetic use). Exposure may dissipate what mere counter-prejudice cannot. The attitudes may already be too familiar, though there is not space enough to dissect all the attitudes whose contemporary effect has been malign.

The deepest aesthetic prejudice is the prejudice against aesthetics, the almost pathological fear of exploring the basis of art.

> I'm not that conscious of what I'm doing, and I have very few theories—I don't know if I have any—about poetry. . . .

But I'm not really that conscious of my own poetry and I'm not sure I want to be.

Philip Levine (1974)

For some of us, the less said about the way we do things the better. And I for one am not even sure that I have a recognizable way of doing things, or if I did that I could talk about it.

Mark Strand (1978)

I don't want to know how I write poetry. Poetry is dangerous: talking too much about it, like naming your gods, brings bad luck.

Margaret Atwood (1971)

Most writers are reserved about naming their art, and it is not merely terror of the inarticulate—not many people will take a scalpel to their wrists to learn about musculature. But if the danger was not felt by Sidney or Dryden, Coleridge or Shelley, Pound or Eliot, it cannot be intrinsic to poetry, as Strand admits in his admonitory condition, *for some of us.* The real fear cannot be named, lest it take vengeance on the namer. (Margaret Atwood pronounces the tetragrammaton *bad luck* instead of writer's *block.*)

In their hostility to aesthetics, many poets believe poetry is the golden egg and poets the geese dissection will not explain, only destroy. This dread of devastating the sources of art measures their awe for their poems, and the ignorance they are willing to endure to preserve that awe. Many poets would accept unconsciousness (to be "not that conscious") or silence ("the less said . . . the better") rather than analyze the impulse of invention.

There is appeasement in denial. Having supplicated whatever irascible gods happen to be listening, Levine and Strand answer (in the interviews from which these passages have been taken) innumerable questions regarding their practice. Their hesitation is not disingenuous. The half-apologetic terms in which it is offered mark the magnitude of their discomfort and how, like superstition, it retains a hold over reason after pretending to be mastered by it.

I just know when I feel the line should break. I used to say
that my criterion for a line of poetry was that it should
have at least two interesting things in it.

John Ashbery (1983)

Contemporary poets trust their feeling before their reason,
and this Romantic reliance on intuition has for so long been the
strength of modern poetry it has become the greatest weakness
as well. Ashbery states an aesthetic principle when he denies its
existence; though negation may mimic the characteristic move-
ment of his poetry, it signifies how weak a force intuition is, how
subject to denial, how contingent on suspicion. If someone *just
knows* when he feels a line should break, he knows nothing
securely. The break cannot be predicted; it must be felt at the
moment of its occurrence.

This is a conscious refusal of conscious style. Though the
enjambment of most free verse may be reduced to a few prin-
ciples, poets are reluctant to do so, at least for their own work.
It's as if free verse provided a permanent state of Keatsian nega-
tive capability, allowing the poet to exist in doubts as long as he
refused to examine his habits. This reduces poetry to a form of
magic. The rejection of rationality, not easy to explain without
recourse to history or sociopathology, recalls the belief that to
analyze Shakespeare corrupts the pleasure of reading him.

The anxiety over analysis is allied to the anxiety of influence—
in the first instance the cost is pleasure; in the second, artistic
freedom.

I am not conscious of having been influenced by anybody
and have purposely held off from reading highly mannered
people like Eliot and Pound so that I should not absorb
anything, even unconsciously.

Wallace Stevens (1954)

To be influenced is to be possessed, and therefore demonic.
The prejudice against reading, common among young poets, is
beguiling in a poet like Stevens, whose work exerts such a fierce
gravitational pull. Most poets would be embarrassed to admit
they cannot enjoy reading poetry, though I have heard another
poet, one of the better of his generation, confess over baked

chicken he had never read Elizabeth Bishop for fear of being influenced. Stevens notes that this is self-denial, not lack of interest.

> Only poets are really interested in poetry. The time to read poetry is before you start to write it; after you start to write it you are afraid to read other people's poetry. . . . In fact, there is probably no one who reads less poetry than I do. It takes very little to make people say that you nourish yourself on the work of other people and, since it is the easiest thing in the world to pick up something unintentionally, the safest plan is not to read other poets.
> *Wallace Stevens (1945)*

Here the implicit good is to be original, to owe nothing to the practice of others, at least nothing to contemporaries. Stevens dreads, not the influence of all the poetry he read before he began to write, but a knowledge of contemporaries that would contaminate his invention of the self (the work of lesser or less-mannered contemporaries was not so poisonous—as his letters make plain, Stevens shied from Eliot, Pound, and Lowell, but not Delmore Schwartz or Richard Eberhart). Young poets who have read almost nothing before 1960, and little after, have taken distaste further than Stevens would have thought possible; the desire to write a poetry completely inviolate is the final inheritance of Romantic decadence.

Originality (sometimes flaring into an aesthetics, like Charles Olson's) must embrace doubt, since denial of tradition removes its familiar supports. Stevens managed to be darkly original despite traditional meter, but many poets wish to exist more securely in their doubts. Why is uncertainty something to be cultivated? For many poets, writing is a secret government, bringing chaotic material to order, and this triumph of order is greatest when the prior control of form is absent. When every choice is allowed the poet and none the form, the poet usurps the power of form, even becomes the form. Form must then line by line adapt to the material ("FORM IS NEVER MORE THAN AN EXTENSION OF CONTENT"—Olson, citing Robert Creeley)—the ordering is therefore always in doubt. To reduce free verse to principles would be to allow its prediction.

A poet's principles may be highly predictable, but only willful perversity could allow poets to conceal *from themselves* their mastery of technique (as Mark Strand recognizes: "I would be kidding myself if I believed that nothing continuous existed in the transactions between myself and my poems. I suppose this is what we mean by craft"). Protection from the knowledge of one's prejudice, a prejudice that might be called technique, can lead to static repetition (the worst plagiarism is self-imitation), and repetition to the artistic decay ignorance was meant to avoid. Despite our tendency to idolize the "original," conventions are as evident in contemporary poetry as in the poetry of other periods; the precise tone, logic, progress of narrative, and affect of our poetry is often as *de rigueur* as the repetitions of a villanelle.

> It's best to write about things close to one's heart, if one wishes to write accurately.
>
> *David Ignatow (1955)*

A Romantic self-reliance demands self-knowledge violently at odds with the metrical and rhythmic ignorance of contemporary poetry (Keats and Byron and Shelley saw no conflict between the strict employments of form and the easy employments of self). Those who place so much emphasis on self-knowledge place little on knowledge of craft—as if the one were morally superior to the other, as if intimacy with the latter could never enhance comprehension of the former. The affairs of the heart are notoriously narrow and unfortunately more narrow-minded than iambic pentameter.

Ignatow does not mean to be doctrinaire; but the apparent innocence of his formulation, familiar as the admonition to write what you know, skirts the importance of knowing something worth knowing. Many young writers assume that poems are made of whatever they manage haphazardly to experience; and much poetry has become not confession but autobiography (confession requiring some outer standard of behavior), an autobiography that assumes any instance in a life is worthy of dramatic note. Few moments are—and of them birth is what we cannot recall and death what we will not be able to remember.

Ignatow's assertion, in its subtle prejudice against intellect, encourages not the maturing of attitude but the retailing of incident. Are there no subjects with intellectual but not emotional fascination? Further, are we able to write most *accurately* about subjects in which we are emotionally involved? Most movingly, perhaps—but accuracy may want a distance not available to those with emotions. Poetry does not have to be honest, or even true; but much of what we accept as sincere is all too devious and false-hearted.

> Poetry must sing or speak from authentic experience. Of all the streams of civilized tradition with roots in the paleolithic, poetry is one of the few that can realistically claim an unchanged function and a relevance which will outlast most of the activities that surround us today. Poets, as few others, must live close to the world that primitive men are in: the world, in its nakedness, which is fundamental for all of us—birth, love, death; the sheer fact of being alive.
>
> *Gary Snyder (1967)*

We might have more to learn from inauthentic experience, if we could discover what exactly that might be. The inauthentic could be said to be literary; that is, derived secondhand from experience. I don't understand in what way the myths of "primitive" poetry can be authentic and not literary. Does Snyder believe that primitive man conversed with animals, was visited by supernatural beings, or witnessed, perhaps, the creation of the world? "Primitive" poetry often seems to rely on highly artificial language and sophisticated literary invention.

Grant that primitive poetry derives from "authentic" experience and is not literary contrivance or the description of ritual. Why *must* poets live close to the world of primitive man? If poets like Snyder abandon the mnemonic devices, the rhyme and meter, at the heart of primitive poetry, why can't other poets find subjects not limited to "birth, love, death"? It is our subtle education, our willingness to appreciate an irregular rhythm, that permits the existence of free verse. Our civilized complexity might allow the elaboration of subject as well—perhaps to include the politics or science primitive man knew little of. Even there, we must be wary of glibly embracing what we do not understand.

> It is similar to what must have been the early feelings of Einstein toward the laws of Isaac Newton in physics. Thus from being fixed, our prosodic values should rightly be seen as only relatively true. Einstein had the speed of light as a constant—his only constant—What have we? Perhaps our concept of musical time.
>
> *William Carlos Williams (1948)*

> The closed, contained quality of such forms has less relation to the relativistic sense of life which unavoidably prevails in the late twentieth century than modes that are more exploratory, more open-ended.
>
> *Denise Levertov (1979)*

Due to science, the physical circumstance of our lives has altered over the centuries, though the attentive visitor to Herculaneum will see how little. Is the fondest romance of our time, however, that our lives are intimately and directly transformed by the theories of science? Levertov might spend a week in Elizabethan England before talking with so much confidence of "the relativistic sense of life" in our late century. The tempting correlations between the science of an era and its art are rarely grounded in more than ingenuity or fantasy. Are our lives more relative because of Einstein or uncertain because of Heisenberg? Scientific theory may modify the way scientists view reality in the laboratory; but out on the sidewalk, even for most scientists, life can be remarkably Ptolemaic and Euclidean.

A vague understanding of science allows the inexact, metaphoric use of scientific terms (something scientists, who love language games, do little to discourage when they name their quarks *charm* and *strange* or, more pointedly, *truth* and *beauty*). Theoretical discoveries have an effect on the world; but the effect tends to be more unpredictable and slow-moving than is allowed by the simple equation of a discovery in science and a change in artistic fashion.

It is no accident that Newtonian physics and the
dominance of neo-classicism coincide, nor can it be
accidental that Riemann's non-Euclidean geometry (1854),
Leaves of Grass, and Rimbaud's *Illuminations* (1873?) show
up like bookends flanking *Origin of the Species.*

Reg Saner (1982)

Even if we suppose that scientific theory only identifies a
tendency emerging simultaneously in art (and this would be to
admit that scientists and not artists are the antennae of the
race), we would need more evidence of the influences upon
Whitman and Rimbaud, as well as of their intentions, before
assenting to such fertile whimsy or believing that, in Whitman's
case, Riemann and Darwin had more to do with *Leaves of Grass*
than the Bible or, for later editions, the Civil War. The preju-
dice shrewdly claims from the progress of science a similar and
mirroring progress in art, when either may be subject to fashion.
Newtonian physics, were they newly enunciated by Sir Isaac to-
morrow, could be used to explain the verse of John Ashbery; but
fashions change somewhat faster than theory.

But I do feel that there are few poets today whose
sensibility naturally expresses itself in the traditional forms
(except for satire or pronounced irony), and that those
who do so are somewhat anachronistic.

Denise Levertov (1979)

Prejudice easily holds a sneer. It is convenient to mistake
fashion for progress, when the fashion happens to be your own.
The word *naturally* is a land mine; but, even if we take Levertov
to mean "effortlessly" rather than "by instinct," the sensibility
would be an odd one that considers love or anger awkward in
meter but irony or satire natural. Few poets could register in
form so complex a mental attitude as irony without being able
to accommodate some of the simple states of love. Levertov may
mean that satire and irony are contrived mental states, that
contrivance requires the artifice of form. The implications of
her sentence are more prescriptive—in artifice, she seems to
say, only artifice belongs. It would not take a great shift of sensi-

bility to find highly artificial the "natural" expressions of our poetry—or to find natural what today seems artificial.

> The distinction between form as prison and form as wildness may correspond to a distinction between kinds of forms, in particular, the mechanical and the organic. The one form would be drawn from human economy, the other from the economy of nature.
>
> *Robert Bly (1981)*

It is a polemical belief, that form constricts rather than liberates. Whether the antecedents of the organic theory lie in Emerson's "Ask the fact for the form" or Coleridge's "The form is mechanic when on any given material we impress a predetermined form. . . . The organic form, on the other hand, is innate" (or further back in Plato, Aristotle, or Plotinus), the uses to which the nineteenth century put the notion were different from those of the twentieth. It has now become an argument against meter or rhyme, not merely against the common forms of poetic tradition. Like most aesthetic prejudices, it supports the felt demands of practice, not metaphysical belief (though the two can occasionally be confused).

> [Iambic pentameter] somehow seems to falsify poetry for me. It has an order of its own that is foreign to nature.
>
> *John Ashbery (1983)*

> In an attempt to write a poem that would be perfectly natural . . . I can't imagine how I would do it in rhyme now.
>
> *Louis Simpson (1973)*

> I can say that we distrust rhyme because it sounds a little tinny, a little false, a little decorative, and a little unnatural.
>
> *Mark Strand (1971)*

The natural is only what we are accustomed to and perhaps has little to do with whether the sonnet can be found in nature or if flowers are metrical. At least until natural selection, or bioengineering, supplies us with a botany of iambs and dactyls, we are unlikely to search the forest for the form. This is Aristotelian mimesis taken to insulting conclusion (as are attempts to found prosody in breath, or meter in the heartbeat). Our language is artificial, a sign-making we cannot find elsewhere in nature, except by simplistic analogy. If we are allowed poems of language, we cannot then be denied the other artifices of intelligence and ingenuity. The raw sophistications of form have been the province of poets who could not be accused of academicism, the academy not having existed in pre-Homeric Greece, say, or barbarian Europe. Rhyme and meter are derived from properties of language, and work best when the proprieties of language are observed (meter cannot effectively cross accent, nor rhyme stray too far from homeoteleuton). Only sophistry would allow one manmade tool and not others—are the knife and the ax legitimated by age but not the computer?

Poetry is under no compulsion to deny the pleasure and effectiveness of form. A fulfillment of stricture, and structure, is a mental rather than moral discipline. The belief, implicit in Beat aesthetics and elsewhere, that poetic form somehow embodies a special political or moral posture is not merely absurd, it is vicious. If free verse conferred on its maker a liberal outlook, Pound would not have been a fascist, nor Eliot an anti-Semite. Should style, the product of forces in fashion and culture, reflect political philosophy? Style is only a corrective. Content is what informs. The idea that the most prosaic style is the most democratic (since any figure or regular rhythm is an artifice imposed on common speech) has been poisonous. It rewards those least engaged by the technical possibilities of their art. Worse, it condescends to an audience whose popular culture consists almost entirely of rigidly stylized drama, and music whose lyrics would in meter and rhyme be recognizable to Campion. The way to reach a popular audience is through the sentiment of content, not that of form.

If poetry is to make nothing happen, it must be very serious indeed. Current free verse, with all its weary prose virtues, no longer engages our blind intelligence, and to that degree is sentimental; it not only fails to test its reader, it fails to test its author. To wish for the return of classical virtues in art would be chimerical; but surely it is time to cut the throat of what Christopher Ricks calls "Romanticism's pathos of self-attention, its grounded pity for itself."

> After a period of getting away from the traditional forms, comes a period of curiosity in making new experiments with traditional forms. This can produce very good work if what has happened in between has made a difference: when it's not merely going back, but taking up an old form, which has been out of use for a time, and making something new with it.
>
> *T. S. Eliot (1959)*

> I think the artist should master all known forms and systems of metric, and I have with some persistence set about doing this.
>
> *Ezra Pound (1918)*

Fashion is deeper than *haute couture*. It is the succession of tensions internal to art, tensions implicated in the very choices any work makes—the denials that are affirmations, the affirmations that are denials. As free verse has played out the impetus of its opposition in 1915 and 1955, between *Cathay* and *Howl*, meter and rhyme have become, in their fashion, and as a fashion, and from out of fashion, the opposition within.

The subversion of fashion has causes, but the causes are intricate and arguable. Perversity and whim may not be least among them. Some of the statements quoted here imply that an aesthetic is perfect and immutable. All aesthetics are contingent, existing at the sufferance of their disciples and their awkward age. To future readers the poems of warring disciplines may seem indistinguishable. The collapse of strategies and rage for the new, which we know as Boredom, murders more fashions than the banner of artistic principle—beside it most statements on aesthetics are pretty rationalizations. Boredom is the ally of great poetry. It will eventually make the unreadable unread.

Behind many of these aesthetic positions lurks the heritage of a debased Romanticism. If poetry is to move beyond the impasse of originality, emotion, and organic form, it must again value intellect and prosody, which have recently enjoyed the popularity of smallpox or hepatitis B. There can be no permanence to reaction or revolt. Every change is a temporary liberation; today's subversion is tomorrow's dogma, to be overthrown in its turn. The reemergence of form among younger poets reacts against what has gone rancid in contemporary poetry. If Pound were living in a Soho loft and Eliot clerking for Citibank, they would be writing in meter and rhyme.

Language against Fear
Chronicle of the Midseventies

James Tate

The allegiance James Tate announced in *The Lost Pilot* (1967), his first book, was to a surrealism that would inform and interpret the familiar. His subsequent work has frequently been an admission of failure, an acknowledgment that nothing, not even surrealism, will work any longer—that language, or communication, its bastard son, has become impossible. *Viper Jazz* opens with an aporia, a confession of limitation:

> I don't know about the cold.
> I am sad without hands.
> I can't speak for the wind
> which chips away at me.

The world has shrunk to that central "I," and each of those sentences, those sad, short bits of prose, admits either an irrecoverable loss or a failure of knowledge. These poems are most comfortable with *nothing*, that ghost, that vacuum; indeed, as a section of one poem defines it:

> It is a tiny obscure lighthouse
> for serious travellers of the night
> whose only vocation
> is to gradually discover a spot
> to root their lonely wardrobes.

It is typical of Tate's perversity to define absence in the terms of presence, but he has always been devoted to the conjugation of opposites: the surreal with the real, the colloquial with the serious, entropy with energy. His non sequiturs sometimes turn into violently yoked aphorisms. More than any of his books, *Viper Jazz* celebrates the notion that no thing may refer to anything else, that the lines of communication are all down. Nothing is certain: "My wife will think I don't love her. / My beautiful wife! / Or was it my mother?"

Viper Jazz is an uneven book, but Tate's jazzy, improvisatory technique is uneven: moments of virtuosity played against an unforgivable flurry of accretion, a blizzard of one-liners. When the poems succeed, they succeed despite their method, as would the classics if composed by computers. Flirting with the actual despite a marriage to negation, the fortunate poems are startling because of method; and for subject they often claim nothing more than method—they are about their own inability to communicate.

Tate has the charm of a brittle intelligence. These new poems give up inhibition for a pregnancy impossible when the subject shapes the form. Theirs is a reckless struggle against language, against subject—against the looming failure at the heart of poetry. Tate's poems have few of the skills of poetry, but many of prose, and they are often as ill-written as prose. Tate is incomprehensible ("Smothered in camouflage of hangdog shy her tiny limp / thunder") and incoherent ("And by rubbing granite cliffs together / morning becomes Thor Heyerdahl / on his way to work"), merely silly ("The zebras want to visit Chicago") and banal ("I must say goodbye / . . . to the fishermen who use their hearts as bait"). His lunacy and slapstick, however, throw the reader off guard and allow him to stumble sometimes into a moment quite wonderful:

> In a flophouse
> a man has it out
> with his obsessions:
> he's locked up in a room with them
> for a whole night, what the hell
> make it a lifetime.

In a book of sixty-eight poems, perhaps a dozen pass safely across the thin ice, defeating the negation they are formed from. "A Voyage from Stockholm," "Liaisons," "A Radical Departure," "Many Problems," "A Box for Tom," and "Disease" imply in their titles the connections, physical and social, that are the circuits of their success. Otherwise, it is just one damned poem after another, a hell of small conceptions and maniacal blithering.

Constance Urdang

"Outside the circle around the campfire / beyond where the lamplight reaches" is where Constance Urdang's fears lurk. This is a poetry not of things but of presences, a habitation in emptiness, or by emptiness. The world outside the campfire repels the seeker, but lures her on. "No! I don't want to see it," she says, even as she sees it, and describes it with the care that tells us at fear's root lies desire—the ability to alter is the presence within things. Of a stick of firewood, she says,

> I think I can read in it
> how hard it is to live
> and how every morning
> the sun creates himself all over again
> and crawls awkwardly over the rim of the world

Transformation is desired because to alter is to begin again, dreaded because all change presages death. "If only there were some adventure other than death," she writes (rather implausibly) on a window. These poems exist in death to the exclusion of everything else (which, of course, death is). From repetition the word, like a lover's name, loses its mortal pressure and becomes mere sound. Suddenly one wonders what "deth" signifies, as one wonders what might be meant by "blud," "bōnz," "stärz," "emp·tē·nes," her other empty nouns.

These are the repetitions of ceremony, litany, the incantation of language against fear. The lines are kept short, since nothing matters except the getting said, the getting out: "let there be no more owners / and no more ownership / no more plats lots liens mortgages / let there be no property." And no properties. Punctuation is often scrapped, so the poems run on—they are fairly unstoppable. Everything must be said before it can be unsaid, undone. At their best, the poems toss overboard the extraneous cargo to keep the ship above water. At worst, they hurl the dreck in all directions: "They believe in Juicy Fruit Gum. / They believe in Hollywood. / They believe in the Fourth of July. / They believe in Dick Tracy."

This nakedness is both beautiful and horrible; but the unclothed lacks the mysterious power of the clothed. The topless

15

waitress is soon just another waitress, no more remarkable than the soup. Even deprived of clothing, the poems are intensely, even aggressively, private. The landscapes are all interiors, though trees, grass, and animals are elaborately carted in and arranged.

The means of *The Picnic in the Cemetery* are finally too limited, the concerns too private to transmute the matter, to turn metamorphosis into metaphysics. There are fine lines mapping out the terrain of sexuality; but compared to the poems of Adrienne Rich, which chart similar regions not so morbidly, Urdang's work is imitative, less complex, and less moving.

Leonard Nathan

The distance from *The Day the Perfect Speakers Left* (1969) to Leonard Nathan's *Returning Your Call* seems a leap into second childhood. The former was urbane, pedantic, disdainful of display; the latter is a hodgepodge of stances, a wild disgorgement of fright and fervor. Between the writing of these books came the rise and decline of the "counterculture," a phenomenon to which not all professors were immune. These new poems have the uneasy, apologetic style of a man not entirely comfortable in his nakedness.

> Which reminds me: I'm Leonard Nathan whose grandpa
> Changed his last name—too Jewish.

> I'm not Leonard Nathan. I'm hiding
> Down here and have fooled the psychiatrists.

What was circumspect is now chatty, and all portraits strain toward self-portrait; all reference, self-reference ("Miss America, this here / Is your beautiful friend, / The middle-aged poet").

The poet awoke one morning, it seems, with a double identity. One identity is political—it doesn't speak, it shouts: "Asia? I don't want Asia. / For God's sake, keep Asia quiet!" Occasionally history freezes into a terrible moment:

> Where at last we stride through foam under torches
> Toward the shut shore to find there
> Someone who looks like you, stripped,

> Wrists tied to her belly, staring out
> Over the senseless black waters.

Too often we judge, not history, but an interpreting voice self-conscious and full of self-interest.

The other identity—personal—also staggers from posture. Here the distance from Death ("Grandpa scares me holding his breath. / His last address was an oxygen tent") and from Beauty ("I tell Beauty, at Her most loving, to shut up") betrays a man insecure with all forms of the Ideal. Though constantly talking, Nathan can never own up to simple Friendship, or Love, or Lust. The few lines of serious intent ("What is said to women has lost / Its silken under-meaning, its rendezvous / Of silence beyond itself, yes / The mere opposite of mere no") are lost to the clowning or whining.

Most of the verse in this book has little to say, or no way to express itself—the language is gathered into a loose, comfortable American prose, the kind cats and dogs can write, though the lines have been violently enjambed to transmit a little shock. "Someday," Nathan writes in this, his sixth collection, "I'm going to speak / In my own voice."

Robert Hayden

Offered again the chance to erase, silently, the early errors and excesses, Robert Hayden has retained all but two of the poems that formed his 1966 *Selected Poems*. This is a poet secure about the past and the past work. In eight new poems and the bulk of two interim volumes, *Angle of Ascent* gradually reveals a shift from narrative to symbolism. The stories have broken down entirely into words, some of rich personal association: "Plowdens, Finns, / Sheffeys, Haydens, / Westerfields. // Pennsylvania gothic, / Kentucky homespun, / Virginia baroque." The resistant spareness of the new poems rewards the hard-edged radiance of memory. Of a night-blooming cereus:

> Lunar presence,
> foredoomed, already dying,
> it charged the room
> with plangency

> older than human
> cries, ancient as prayers
> invoking Osiris, Krishna,
> Tezcátlipóca.

Hayden exploits the classics and the contemporary, historical anecdote and personal encounter; what grants history poignancy—that it cannot be changed—also gives pathos to the personal. His explorations of slave history include swatches of song and dialect, not impenetrable anger or voguish posture. His homages are to Mark Van Doren as well as Malcolm X; the poems conjure up lives caught in the desperation of poverty, or of decadence. His difficult feelings for the era that began with the arrival of slaves in America and ended with the Civil War and Reconstruction produce his most serious poems, including "The Dream," "The Ballad of Sue Ellen Westerfield," and the stunning "Middle Passage."

"Middle Passage" is a deceptive and perfectly modulated pastiche, its voices contained in diary, deposition, and reminiscence, its subject the slave trade, the "voyage through death / to life upon these shores."

> Sails flashing to the wind like weapons,
> sharks following the moans the fever and the dying;
> horror the corposant and compass rose.
> ....
> *Deep in the festering hold thy father lies,*
> *of his bones New England pews are made,*
> *those are altar lights that were his eyes.*
> ....
>   "A plague among
> our blacks—Ophthalmia: blindness—& we
> have jettisoned the blind to no avail.
> It spreads, the terrifying sickness spreads.
> Its claws have scratched sight from the Capt.'s eyes
> & there is blindness in the fo'c'sle."

As "Shuttles in the rocking loom of history, / the dark ships move, the dark ships move"; the mingled tales, the mortal terrors, display the moral blindness at slavery's heart, the self-interest that destroys the self. "Middle Passage" is a poem on slavery without contemporary rival, but finally a singular performance whose special construction (heavily indebted to *The Waste Land*) did not invite imitation.

Hayden's later poems have not discovered other means rich enough to encompass public or private history. Their defects include compositional tics (repetitions, for example: "the name he never can he never can repeat") and, especially in the newer poems placed first in the book, occasional opaqueness. At worst the phrases break up, the words fly apart, and the associative structure holds no meaning—the poems shatter into beautiful images. As the older poems drape themselves in description and narrative, the newer seem insubstantial.

Derek Walcott

"That sail which leans on light, / tired of islands, / a schooner beating up the Caribbean // for home" reveals the acuity of Derek Walcott's vision, the terrifying precision combined with fresh metaphorical invention. Do we not see, he asks in effect, because we must see

> When the cows are statues in the misting field
> that sweats out the dew,
> and the horse lifts its iron head
> and the jaws of the sugar mules
> ruminate and grind like the factory?

Sight, our frailest sense, detects the decay that is the world. Any beauty may have a shabby element: "Sunset, the cheapest of all picture-shows, / was all they waited for; old men like empties / set down from morning outside the almshouse." To confront us with the seen, Walcott reveals the force of the tawdry, the cheap, the broken-down. Everywhere his metaphors pull the world to themselves: "Desolate lemons, hold / tight, in your bowl of earth, / the light to your bitter flesh." Only things seen, not in the right light or the wrong light, but in a light that quickens them, can rise from the page, neither mirage nor miracle. Walcott, ever interested in the intimate, outlines the local gravity that arranges objects about an object:

> The chapel, as the pivot of this valley,
> round which whatever is rooted loosely turns—
> men, women, ditches, the revolving fields

of bananas, the secondary roads—
draws all to it, to the altar
and the massive altarpiece.

Visual and religious power are related; all our religions are based on optical transactions, the supernatural made natural, and seen.

Though he may stay in the Chelsea Hotel or fly to Los Angeles, Walcott's home is the Caribbean. He walks "Down the dead streets of sun-stoned Frederiksted, / the first free port to die for tourism," where the people and landscape bear down on imagination. Everywhere he registers the losses: lovers, honor, simplicity. Only the imagination is fixed; and when Walcott writes of poets and poetry, it is with vigor and freshness that overcome their limitations as subjects. The writers he invokes— Neruda, Mandelstam, Joyce, Conrad—have widened the possibilities of the immutable. Other tributes lie discreetly in image: to Auden ("like walking sheaves of harvest, the quick crowd / thickened in separate blades of cane or wheat") and the Cranes, Hart ("like the dice / of skulls rolling over / the tilting seafloor") and Stephen ("I stood on the sand, I saw / black horsemen"). He invents his Adam, Aeneas, and Odysseus, even while realizing "The classics can console. But not enough."

So many of his metaphors are of light, it is no wonder Walcott's torture is Promethean ("we were all netted to one rock / by vines of iron, our livers / picked by corbeaux and condors / in the New World"). Titanic talent embitters, because it perceives its limitations. It is just the embittered note, the arrogance that flaws the music of these poems, that recovers from the classical and the beautiful the merely human. There is no poem in *Sea Grapes* that does not repay rereading. Walcott's occasional rhyme is muted; it exerts only a slight pull at the lines, and controls their tides. Such poetry transfers to us a sudden respect for the word and the world; under its influence we become more generous. I have no faith that readers agree absolutely on which poets achieve such music; but if there is magic in language, it is in poems that wed the passion of elegy or self-dissection to rival complexities of tone and sound. Walcott is one of a dozen or so poets writing in English who deserve constant and informed attention.

Two Countries

Robert Penn Warren

Having outlived most of the poets of his own generation and the generation after, at seventy-five Robert Penn Warren is writing with the ferocious energy of his old age. The anxieties of aging structure and subvert his poems, the risks of sentiment occasionally overcome by the rewards of serenity. Serenity is perhaps too composed a word to describe the momentary seizures of peace that interrupt these poems. His work is fueled by questions, over 150 in the fifty poems here (the poems are a congress, or a carnival, of rhetorical questions). Warren is not at rest with himself or the world: the press of death urges him onward.

Being Here is an autobiography of spirit, longings present against longings past, the desire of the present for its past. The opening poem recalls a childhood picnic; the closing addresses a passerby on a snowy night, a walk transfigured into life's isolation. Warren is haunted by nature even in dreams:

> All I can dream tonight is an autumn sunset,
> Red as a hayrick burning. The groves,
> Not yet leafless, are black against red, as though,
> Leaf by leaf, they were hammered of bronze blackened
> To timelessness.

Nature anchors these meditations, a nature seemingly timeless, though time-ridden as man: not since Roethke has a poet been so enthralled by his surrounds. Where Roethke wanted to become what he beheld, Warren remains an observer detached from his landscape; that is, a critic. He returns to the same beach he knew as a young man and gauges his life against its durability. He takes his lessons like a good Romantic; there is no realization that beach has shifted or rock crumbled.

Warren is a poet of painterly instinct and visionary ambition:

> Black of grackles glints purple as, wheeling in sun-glare,
> The flock splays away to pepper the blueness of distance.
> Soon they are lost in the tracklessness of air.
> I watch them go. I stand in my trance.

In the "trance of realization" that often follows these moments of vision he forms his philosophy—and a tedious philosophy it is. When he finds a drowned monkey on a beach, when he describes a Civil War veteran or a country funeral, when he recalls a childhood story years later in a different landscape, vision creates a drama to which philosophy is entirely unnecessary.

The authority of these stories descends from Warren's patriarchal tongue, a tongue whose idiosyncracies have the force of cranky individualism. Clausal, phrasal, the diction curiously clipped and the syntax inverted, his style reproduces, better than any poet's since Hopkins, the grammar of seeing:

> Turned, saw,
> Beyond knotting fog-clots, how Chinaward now
> The sun, a dirty pink smudge, grew larger, smokier,
> More flattened, then sank.

The tortured syntax releases a visual world.

This practiced awkwardness, which also mimics the caprice of thinking, is marked less agreeably by bathetic description ("The wet thigh of a nymph, by a spring, agleam where stars peer in"), predictable metaphors, clichés, sententiousness ("All we can do is strive to learn the cost of experience"), and unconscious humor ("Slowly stars, in a gradual / Eczema of glory, gain definition"). How addicted he *is* to stars ("day-star," "first star," "starstung," "starward I stared," "star-tumbling stream," "while stars were black," "star after star") and words like *glory*. From a poet of intellect he has become a poet of instinct, whose skill now founders on sensation as once it foundered on form.

It is hard to estimate how much of a poet's view is an accident of his health, his age, or his household. One critic wrote of *Being Here* that it shows what happens—this was a favorable review— when a poet survives beyond ambition. Yet this book is eaten up with ambition, from the lengthy list of Warren's awards and achievements to the coy, ill-considered "Afterthought," where he tries to justify in prose what he should have finished in poetry. His unsureness about the book's unity rivals his unease over the weakness of the parts.

These poems are full of talk, the best of it inspired storytelling, the worst a pretentious musing on Time, Truth, and old age. If the better poems find their subject in Warren's youth and their style in his fiction, the worst issue from his age and his criticism. His animations (what poet isn't a petty god?) are more interesting than his analysis: the swift drama of vision pales the trudge of his philosophy.

Since the late sixties, Warren has written as though each poem were his last. The manner is flat-out, frightened, often quite beautiful (there is beauty in a man's admission of fear). The title *Being Here* bears the feverish surprise of survival. Even the staging of these poems—Warren alone, or Warren reminiscing about a moment of transcendent apartness—invites the premonition of death. Perhaps if he could overcome the nightmare of death at his door, Warren could write poems of real tranquillity and knowledge. But it is ill-natured to suggest a man give up his gratitude.

Seamus Heaney

The guarded grace and mastery of Seamus Heaney's *Field Work* (1979) has prompted his publisher to collect his four earlier books of poetry and to issue simultaneously a volume of his prose. Though he writes in English and publishes in London, Heaney is the most Irish of poets, less by heritage or landscape than by a central estrangement—he is, as he says, an "inner émigré."

Heaney's early poems were taken from country material. From home life and farm life come the blackberry picking, the milk churning, the kitten drowning, the usual chores and sorrows of childhood. The poetry in *Poems: 1965–1975* wants these moments to have transumptive rigor, the crush of blackberries "Leaving stains upon the tongue," the dead kittens representing "The Early Purges." When the metaphorical value is so narrow, the poems, though delicately weighted and written with great verbal gift, are stale with their own composition.

Heaney is fascinated with the terms of his vocation; and his poems refer frankly to the writer's work, the labor over words. His sense of land and history is yoked to language, the "vowel-meadow" and the "iron / flash of consonants / cleaving the line," so that his deep, almost erotic regard for nature parallels a sensual love of word:

> White pocks
> Of cockle, blanched roofs of clam and oyster
> Hoard the moonlight, woven and unwoven
> Off the bay. At the far rocks
> A pale sud comes and goes.

As the erotic is often alien, so is the language: *pampooties, mizzling, docken, rath, bullaun.* The odd, dialectical words Heaney lavishes upon his poems create the surface difficulty of landscape. They intrude less on home scenes and local figures— the salmon fisher, the blacksmith, the thatcher (simple figures in a complex land?). These figures have their own mystic force, a force of being, felt even in the homely services of an unlicensed bull:

> He circled, snored and nosed. No hectic panting,
>
> Just the unfussy ease of a good tradesman;
> Then an awkward, unexpected jump, and
>
> His knobbled forelegs straddling her flank,
> He slammed life home, impassive as a tank,
>
> Dropping off like a tipped-up load of sand.

Part irony, part pathos, the contrast between the bull's attitude and act is typical of Heaney's work. Recurrent in his poetry are the need for life's secret ceremonies and the passion for secrets a land retains. His most resonant images cleave to the bodies dug from Jutland bogs—the bog people, strangled before pagan gods or executed for unknown crimes, whose blackened, mummified corpses prefigure the "Stockinged corpses / Laid out in the farmyards," Ireland's new violently dead.

From the solidity of his early poems—written to confirm his gifts within daily observance or nightly reading—comes, mysteriously perhaps, the sudden shudder of human affairs in the last poems of *North* (1975), the book that led directly to *Field Work.* There is a loosening of spirit in this work, as if like Antaeus (who figures in two poems) Heaney had been freed from the earth that was source of strength and prison both; but Antaeus's defeat is for Heaney a victory. The monologue of the mind gives way to conversation, the lockstep of composition submits to natural expression (though this may be a more diabolic composition):

This morning from a dewy motorway
I saw the new camp for the internees:
A bomb had left a crater of fresh clay
In the roadside, and over in the trees

Machine-gun posts defined a real stockade.
There was that white mist you get on a low ground
And it was déjà-vu, some film made
Of Stalag 17, a bad dream with no sound.

Is there a life before death? That's chalked up
In Ballymurphy. Competence with pain,
Coherent miseries, a bite and sup,
We hug our little destiny again.

The prose in *Preoccupations* offers different access to the poet's imagination. For those who find in biography the sources of poetry, two essays supply Heaney's rural childhood and his later residence in Belfast. Of more consequence are the lectures that, while perusing the work of other poets (Wordsworth, Yeats, Hopkins), let Heaney discuss his craft. He is one of the few poets who can speak with engaging intelligence about the makings of his art. Though these lectures, essays, talks, and reviews often strain against their origins, they give him opportunity to develop, if not a theory, at least a pragmatics of poetry.

Among poets in the British Isles, Heaney has placed himself with Ted Hughes, Philip Larkin, and Geoffrey Hill—that is, among the finest poets in the language. Subject to the conflict of privacy and politics, of personal revelation and public avowal, his work dramatizes the contradiction central to the serious poetry of our age: "On the one hand, poetry is secret and natural, on the other hand it must make its way in a world that is public and brutal."

Overseas and Under

Though they belong to distinct cultures—Philip Levine is American; Geoffrey Hill, British; and Derek Walcott, West Indian—these poets borrow and continue the major traditions of English poetry. Born within two years of 1930, they are now at the height of their careers. Some of the extraordinary poetry of the next decade should be written by them, and each addition to their labor can be ignored by no one who cares about modern poetry.

Derek Walcott

Derek Walcott's work is exquisitely crafted without being fussy. He observes with a dedication driven, not to record the world exactly, but to render it unforgettable:

> strop on these goggles, I'll guide you there myself.
> It's all subtle and submarine,
> through colonnades of coral,
>
> past the gothic windows of sea fans
> to where the crusty grouper, onyx-eyed,
> blinks, weighted by its jewels, like a bald queen.

Sight is his primary sense and satisfaction. His language, so rich it deserves extensive quotation impossible here, never wrenches or strains for effect—it is all effect. His natural images have an enriching passion, but it is sometimes the passion of Tiffany's.

The Star-Apple Kingdom concentrates on the Caribbean, his "history-orphaned islands" harboring the displaced and dispossessed. The most striking new poems dramatize the lives of men poisoned by their pasts. In "Koenig of the River," a disillusioned adventurer reckons his losses. His companions have drowned at sea, and the kingdom he would conquer (*koenig* = king) has shrunk to an insignificant stream. In "The Schooner *Flight*," a mulatto sailor returns to the sea, where a storm gives him release from the land and the woman he left. A high care for the music of speech heightens these poems—in the latter, a monologue, native dialect becomes poetic idiom:

> Out in the yard turning gray in the dawn,
> I stood like a stone and nothing else move
> but the cold sea rippling like galvanize
> and the nail holes of stars in the sky roof.

If there are lapses in Walcott's work, they come from attempting too much. His sailor says lamely at one point, "Either I'm nobody, or I'm a nation"; at another, "I had no nation now but the imagination." There is also the danger of settling for the pictorial; Walcott is so gifted at the seen he can become merely an observer, reveling in detachment. Nevertheless, these ten new poems—some very ambitious—represent composition of a sustained order. Few contemporaries are his equal.

Geoffrey Hill

Geoffrey Hill's poetry has received sometimes outlandish praise from critics ("the monumental English poet of the latter 20th century"), but that should not be held in his disfavor. His work in *Tenebrae,* after the relative clarity of *Mercian Hymns* (1971), has returned to the knotted rhetoric of his earlier poems to record a man's endeavor for grace, the contention between desire for salvation and withdrawal from commitment.

> Crucified Lord, you swim upon your cross
> and never move. Sometimes in dreams of hell
> the body moves but moves to no avail
> and is at one with that eternal loss.
>
> You are the castaway of drowned remorse,
> you are the world's atonement on the hill.
> This is your body twisted by our skill
> into a patience proper for redress.

Few poets are able to charge words with Hill's power, and here that power reinforces a struggle with his God that is tormented, obdurate, and frequently mysterious. A reader may rail against a poet's crabbed intensity, may consider that Hill cowers behind a veil of language; but his clotted speech has the inevitability of its dark tragedy. What has been said could have been said in no better way.

In Hill as in Donne, there is a crucial transaction between religious and erotic love, between passion and possession. This sacred ambiguity turns inward as a wrenching of emotion and outward as projection onto landscape. Hill observes nature acutely:

> The pigeon purrs in the wood; the wood has gone;
> dark leaves that flick to silver in the gust,
> and the marsh-orchids and the heron's nest,
> goldgrimy shafts and pillars of the sun.

There is something self-consciously gnomic, pridefully dense, in such impaction; the real struggle may be not between Hill and his God but between Hill and his pride. Line by line, stanza by stanza, his work gives the pleasure of words freshly used. If this is a Pentecostal tongue, it is a rich and burning addition to our language.

Philip Levine

In Philip Levine's voice there has often been a weary acceptance of the world, the urban, blue-collar world; but concern with his past has turned coercive, his attraction to death become a clue to some conflict only adumbrated in his new work, *7 Years from Somewhere.* The familiar locales—California, Detroit, Spain—appear without the flaring details that gave contrary presence to his recent books. Even the ugliness of Detroit—surely no homelier city ever inspired poetry—now seems indefinite and anonymous. Levine has turned inward, toward a contemplation rooted in plain speech.

This contemplation falls at the onset of middle age, and in many poems Levine watches his younger, receding self—voyeurism is a drama in the strain of self-observation. Levine has always been a poet of compassion; though his tenderness verges on cloying sensitivity (his dedication reads, "This book is for you"), he can smuggle feeling into a poem.

In this new bleakness the lines that crackle are usually where instance sharpens into image: "the sea / the colour of wasted iron riding / up the shore to break over / the fishing boats." Beside technicians of language like Walcott and Hill, Levine's pale colloquialism exerts only a mild lunar pull:

> but we were here, waiting
> because that was all we had
> been brought here for, probably all
> we were good for, and we were good.

Only three words in that passage are more than one syllable in length. The very flatness of the voice has a scary, alienating effect, yet the constant references to aging, the visits to grave-yards, and the sympathy for the dead demonstrate in their dog-gedness not a wish for death but a way to keep on living.

Levine has himself provided the amusing means of judging his past decade by juxtaposing in *Ashes* thirteen poems printed in a small-press edition, *Red Dust* (1971), with nineteen new pieces. The grand disjunctions that moved his earlier poems are gone; the witty insouciance has mostly been ground from his work. What method of arrangement argued that some new work be printed in *7 Years from Somewhere,* the rest here, I cannot determine. Though a few early poems might be mistaken for late, or vice versa, it is relatively easy to assign the poems to recent or distant composition. The weakness in Levine's new poems—and I am not sure that weariness is always weakness—has yet to be transformed by the steady darkening of his vision.

The Present Bought
on the Terms of the Past

Every unhappy imagination is unhappy in its own way. Beneath the elegant expressions of Donald Justice's poetry lies a despair that, however disguised, infuses any act, however heartening. His poetry triumphs over modern desperation, becoming one of our acute imaginative voices; but in the process Justice becomes a modern turned inside out: confession is silenced, revelation masked, statement disavowed.

From his first book, *The Summer Anniversaries* (published in 1960 and perversely titled after a poem uncollected until now),* Justice has stood outside his poems, beyond the scope of action. When his presence intervenes, he has suppressed his individuality, rendered experience as dream or drama, or performed in personae. Given this self-exclusion, the concerns of his first book are remarkably personal: memory, childhood, and the old familial drama. It is in order to discuss the most personal subjects that Justice must set them at a distance. His early poems constitute a family album; but the family includes the mad, the weak, and the lost, lives past their meridian and beyond home. To examine that decaying world, whose myths are the Fall and the curse of Atreus, he is willing to explore the polar regions of thought: madness and dream. "On a Painting by Patient B of the Independence State Hospital for the Insane":

> One sees their children playing with leopards, tamed
> At great cost, or perhaps it is only other children,
> For none of these objects is anything more than a spot,
> And perhaps there are not any children but only leopards
> Playing with leopards, and perhaps there are only the spots.

The bitter wit derives not just from frustration at madness, but from the grim futility of interpreting any work of art. Similarly, the transfiguring dreamscape of "Sestina: A Dream" becomes analogous to the poetic act itself; that is, to the sestina that must

---

*Though similar in structure to the now discarded "Anniversaries."

comprehend and reorder the borrowings of experience. In both poems form revises the inadequate assumptions of a content-ridden self.

Such self-mastering through form could not, perhaps, be long sustained; and in his second book, *Night Light* (1967), the form begins to ravel in favor of content. A new course in art appreciation, contained in "Anonymous Drawing," formulates (as Richard Howard has already noted) a crucial ars poetica. A petty lord has kept an artist waiting, and

> However fast he should come hurrying now
> Over this vast greensward, mopping his brow
> Clear of the sweat of the fine Renaissance morning, it would be
>   too late.
> The artist will have had his revenge for being made to wait,
> A revenge not only necessary but right and clever—
> Simply to leave him out of the scene forever.

To abolish himself from the landscape, to observe only what lies before him, the poet must keep the self, that petty lord, off the premises of the poem or so heavily disguise him that he is not easily identified. To this practice of self-effacement Justice has become devoted. Like doorways into and out of *Night Light,* "Orpheus Opens His Morning Mail" and "Narcissus at Home" introduce just those voices through which the poet can speak— mythic figures shrink-wrapped around the domestic self. In the poetics of indirection, even poems seemingly most personal may derive from foreign originals or the operations of chance. Such games played to engage the imagination provide his forms; the protective self-effacement becomes his subject. For other poets, poetry is the soul's flattering mirror; in Justice the self turns away from the mirror, renouncing self-observation only to write of it obsessively, leaving the mirror empty and hence an obsessive symbol.

The drama of self-exclusion provokes a symbolic reaction— the poet's chafing at the very boundaries he has created. His vengeance on drama, like his vengeance on form, is to transgress what has been announced as limitation; the title of *Departures* (1973), his most mature and most unsettled book, signifies not merely stylistic leave-taking—poetry fragmented, poetry chanced into being, poetry less and less formal—but also psychological rupture and separation. The movement of these poems is not line to line, but from inside to outside, from here to there. The first seven poems of *Departures,* as arranged in *Selected Poems,* concern a mirror, a group of inanimate objects, two vices, a dancer, a crime, an anonymous man, and an assassination. The eighth addresses twenty questions to an unknown entity ("Is there no word for calyx in your tongue?"). The ninth withdraws from its reader. A poetic world has been constructed outside the self no longer intimate with it.

Justice's recourse to emblems of solitude—music and mirrors—is no less significant than his attraction to drama, the disguise of self. An important curtain fall occurs in "Homage to the Memory of Wallace Stevens," in which "The *the* has become an *a.*" Referring to the final line of Stevens's "The Man on the Dump" ("Where was it one first heard of the truth? The the"), the poet laments the particular becoming general, the definite growing indefinite.

> The opera of the gods is finished,
> And the applause is dying.
> . . . .
> What has been good? What has been beautiful?
> The tuning up, or the being put away?
> The instruments have nothing more to say.
> . . . .
> Now all quotations from the text apply,
> Including the laughter, including the offstage thunder,
> Including even this almost human cry.

The last line's self-mocking alienation is appropriate to a symbolic closing that betrays fears of mortality and silence. This withdrawal begets others, but only death is the encore for such absolute self-effacement. For a poet so entranced by blank mirrors, it is curious Justice is not attracted to the demonic Doppelgänger of romance—the vampire. Would it not be an appropriate figure for a poet who has ransacked foreign poets for inspiration—Alberti, Vallejo, Guillevic? To suck another's blood, as poets of fierce appetite know, is to become original; and from his influences—Stevens, Hardy, Auden—Justice has fashioned a compelling voice. For this poet, this consummate gamesman, the most frightening subject, his own death, has been—had to be!—approached through a poetic borrowing, in "Variations on a Text by Vallejo":

> Donald Justice is dead. One Sunday the sun came out,
> It shone on the bay, it shone on the white buildings,
> The cars moved down the street slowly as always, so many,
> Some with their headlights on in spite of the sun,
> And after a while the diggers with their shovels
> Walked back to the graveside through the sunlight,
> And one of them put his blade into the earth
> To lift a few clods of dirt, the black marl of Miami,
> And scattered the dirt, and spat,
> Turning away abruptly, out of respect.

Little poetry immediately followed the disavowals of *Departures*.

The tactical feints Justice employs have allowed his imagination, sufficiently armored, to disclose what it otherwise would conceal: the battle to sustain feeling, to defeat silence. What have been the costs of reticence? First, the loss of self as a foreground subject. Second, a lack of love poems (except of the wryest sort—"Ode to a Dressmaker's Dummy"). Third, a weakness in the poems of pure observation or recollection, whose proper center—the poet affected by his past—is offstage, unavailable to the reader. Such poems do not complete dramatic actions for their meaning. Photographs of the interior, their privacy seals them up.

The disparity, throughout Justice's work, between poems merely observed and poems enacted implies, not that two men wrote them, but that one man wrote at very different levels of imaginative engagement. The poets to whom that higher imagination is most closely allied are Anthony Hecht (in bitter irony) and Elizabeth Bishop (in reserve). Though Justice lacks Hecht's overwhelming (and sometimes overweening) angst or Bishop's little shocks of description, he shares their lunar attention to language, their precise modulations of feeling, the wit they have embedded in form (they also share, of course, the influence of Auden). In addition, Justice has achieved an elegiac intensity, a rueful elegance that heightens the everyday while declaring its frailty. His poetry, unlike the encrusted jewelry box of so many intellective poets, is an intricate watchwork, a mechanism with purpose *(to tell time)*, gears moving in close tolerance. The obliging form of such poetry is forbearance, a withholding of the self from the object of concern without losing sympathetic excitement, a satisfaction not in tragedy but in the surrender to demands the world makes of us all.

Selected Poems has allowed Justice to discard two dozen poems (though, lamentably, such housecleaning has caused the loss of "Narcissus at Home" and "To Satan in Heaven"), to revise poems here and there (to considerable improvement in "Last Days of Prospero"), to rectify sins of omission with half a dozen poems previously uncollected, including a fragment from a long-abandoned long poem, "Bad Dreams," and to add ten new poems, some of unexpected intimacy. In the new poems, Justice has returned from his departures to restrictive forms and a controlling absorption in childhood and memory. From them emerge two of his strongest poems, "First Death" and "Childhood," the latter a poem of extravagant seeing:

> Winter mornings now, my grandfather,
> Head bared to the mild sunshine, likes to spread
> The Katzenjammers out around a white lawn chair
> To catch the stray curls of citrus from his knife.
> Chameleons quiver in ambush; wings
> Of monarchs beat above bronze turds, feasting.

Justice is a poet of loss; to thwart that loss he attempts to remake the past in his poems, a private archaeology preserving what otherwise would vanish. His craft has been to write ever more cunningly of a poet's central concerns: his loss in time, his imaginative gain—the present bought on the terms of the past. Only the spareness of his output and his characteristic self-abnegation have denied him more general recognition.

The eighty-eight titles of *Selected Poems* (a number significant to a poet who would rather have been a pianist) now secures his *made* past, his past as a poet. The chronological arrangement of the poems exposes the character of his advances and retreats—for example, the progressive remission of form in *Night Light*. New typography has considerably enhanced the warmth and vision of his first two books. That vision finds expression in the final line of "Childhood," the final poem in this exquisitely crafted collection—"Forlorn suburbs, but with golden names!" Language may redeem bleakness, even while the poet recognizes the false show such language enacts.

Younger Poets

Marilyn Hacker

Marilyn Hacker's *Presentation Piece* (1974, winner of the National Book Award) and *Separations* (1976) were a violent mixture of classic forms and colloquial sensibility, joining "radical skin, reactionary im- / agination." In her third book, *Taking Notice,* her sensibility has outrun her style. The diction that contained so well her tours de force is ill adapted to dailiness—lists of objects, lines filled flat with existence, desire padded out with descriptions of meals. The forms—sonnets, sestinas, pantoums, canzoni—have become refuge for a distracted imagination; there is now contention between the onslaught of sentence and the Maginot Line of meter.

Too many of these recent poems have no impulse beyond their minor occasions. Lines on starting to write in an art colony, on declining a transatlantic dinner invitation, or composed in the sixteen letters of an LED display board don't have impetus beyond a transient urge to write down, the writer's most dangerous indulgence. Bad poetry is just as bad whether written for a child's birthday or a queen's coronation; the modesty of the occasion confers no charity on it.

The first half of Hacker's new book frames her alienation from men, the second her affair with a woman; but the relief is temporary and hard-won. Undoubtedly the poet felt she could go no further with her formal past; the present book should therefore be viewed as transitional. When she begins her affair, her poems regain their bright authority—the final sequence of twenty-five sonnets is edgy with wit. A marvelous sestina ("From Provence") and a verse letter from Cinderella to her sisters show the sly affections of which Hacker is capable:

> Even his mistress
> —*you* would have assumed he had a mistress—
> gritted her teeth and had me come to lunch
> and whined about the way she was mistreated.
> And I suppose she's right, she was mistreated.

James McMichael

From the dreck of California culture—

>   the spanishy
>   flat shuttered fronts, wrought-iron bars and spears
>   and balconies with canvas awnings, doors with the ornate
>   churrigueresques that public buildings had and
>   movie houses, filling stations, churches, and the stores—

James McMichael has fashioned a two-thousand-line discursive poem that indulges the landscape of childhood within the adult economy of need. Taking the author from Pasadena to Europe, this Wordsworthian project begins with matter and moves slowly into mind, the pressures of psychology replacing those of history.

The rambling disquisition is anchored by history's anecdotes (the Industrial Revolution, California land development) and the minutiae of human ordering (house construction, the parts of the organ, British colonial stamps)—behind them lie the discovery of the "ordinary hidden business." A language flattened by the poet's anxieties—

>   As predicates of what's been well-rehearsed,
>   we're either well- or ill-behaved. To help us know
>   the different points of stress at different times, we're
>   averaged out—

is more engaged by the drama of landscape:

>   The mountain was absurdly
>   vertical and dark, and the cars that passed below it
>   droned in their stupor through the pepper trees.

McMichael has worked diligently (as in his last book, *The Lover's Familiar* [1978]) to refurbish the long prosy poem. But the long poem may depend on an architecture not merely of curious interests or the sociology of the poet's childhood, if that childhood has no more conscience than character. Art is long and life is short, but sometimes the life isn't short enough. If spirit does not have the hard glare of Pasadena (not since Dante, at least), the spirit's weakness is still central to history and perhaps to the willed order of the poetic act.

Alfred Corn

Of these poets Alfred Corn, the most attuned to the natural world, commands the most civilized array of verbal effect. *The Various Light* finds in the landscapes of New England and the ruins of Europe the moral lessons that goad an urban intellect:

> Is hardship renewal? The cold waves
> Keep coming in, little restrained
> By islands offshore, where they ride
> Ringed around by small, stripped-down craft.

This classical awareness moderates its feelings to its forms—a number of the finest poems here are set pieces: "At the Grave of Wallace Stevens," "Reading *Pericles* in New London," "Remembering Mykinai." The sensibility serves him best disrupted by passion or deepened by the summons of vision:

> Nearby, the beehive tomb lay, an underground
> Dome sunk in gloom. Its resonance chilled us, as
> Trapped flies, whose droning stunned the eardrum,
> Sluggishly spiraled above our comments.

The responsive ear and supple vocabulary (the close appearance of *dolby* and *lachrymal* suggest its range) are sometimes wasted in glibness and empty wordplay: "the notions you had had had had . . ." Though at worst Corn bogs down in rendering minutely the evidence or misconstruals of the senses, he does not forget the wider purpose of his words—to join the sensuous world to the horrors of its time: "The dolphin sometimes swims / In oil-stained seas; is it less delphic then?" In such lines *The Various Light,* like his two earlier books, attends to the serious consequences, whether in poetry or in life, of "The candid, casual arrangements made."

In the Extreme

"First books are a plague," an editor once remarked. Week after week they arrive in review offices, in Jiffy bags brown as rats—soon they overrun the place. No one can tell them apart, yet they contain in thinnest form years of hope, imitative desire, intimations of the tragic or the vain—and occasionally a bright spark of feeling. Only a few poets survive them.

Sharon Olds

In *Satan Says,* Sharon Olds relies on an extremity of image and a skillful manipulation of violence, a violence coolly and coldly detached:

> The lady in ruched sateen is lying
> on the Turkey carpet, belly down,
> a dropped seal, a dark pool like
> oil under the face, darkness like
> hair all over the face.
> ("Photographs Courtesy of the Fall River Historical Society")

There is a dead gentleman in the pictures, too, whose "face has been divided into parts, a map, / and broken up like a puzzle." These are only inert images, dead ones, until the final stanza:

> The daughter was let off,
> but as you look at the pictures, the long
> cracks between the sections of his face,
> the back of her skull uneven as some
> internal organ, the conviction is flat.
> Only a daughter could have done that.

It is a dark observation by a poet who sees herself only in terms of others, only in her relations—mother, daughter, sister, lover. She would tease a family from even the most disparate of groups, find in-laws in outlaws, fulfilling some furious need to relate to others only to deny them, to define herself by rejection of the family affair. Denial and rejection are one thing, however; murder is another. Her gruesome interest in these bloody axed bodies, these Bordens, is unexplained until the final line, which seems to expose—in the lethal harmony of that flat rhyme— something horribly private in the author.

The harmony of rhyme is rare in Olds's work. Her poems are crowded with metaphors that upstage what they represent:

> Now the mother is the other one,
> breasts hard bags of rock salt,
> the bluish milk seeping out, her soul
> there in the small carriage, the child in her
> risen to the top, like cream,
> and skimmed off.
>
> ("Young Mothers I")

The mother's alienation from her violated body ought to allow the extenuation of these images; but they exist in such scrupulous isolation the mind is newly distracted as each snaps into position. Then come the embarrassing questions: How do rock-salt breasts exude a blue milk? How is a baby, emerging between its mother's legs, skimmed off the top?

Like any virgin fiancée, Olds has passed the blood test ("streaked with blood," "blood bond," "blood-spattered," "blood-red," "blood bomb," "language of blood," "blood culture," "raised on blood"), dreaming not of marriage but of cutlery ("knife / hanging from my hand," "she / enters the dream of murder, mutilation, her / old self bleeding in pieces on the butcher paper," "my inner sex / stabbed again and again with terrible pain like a knife," "The sky is black as charred wood, / the moon stuck in it like an axe," "sprouts struck out their knives," "that first time / he took his body like a saw to me and / cut through to my inner sex"). The knife is her instrument of the sexes—castrating weapon or lethal penis. It's not so much that she's read Freud—she thinks she *is* Freud.

Olds becomes so lost in the revery of image she forgets that these lives (or these deaths) must be honored:

> The year of the mask of blood, my father
> hammering on the glass door to get in

was the year they found her body in the hills,
in a shallow grave, naked, white as
mushroom, partially decomposed,
raped, murdered, the girl from my class.

("That Year")

It is a carefully modulated beginning; but the murdered class-
mate is immediately abandoned, equated with the dreary events
of puberty and the separation of the poet's parents. Such abuse
of the dead, the little girl a stage prop with rigor mortis, seems a
small misdemeanor when Olds introduces Auschwitz:

There was a word for us. I was: a Jew.
It had happened to six million.
And there was another word that was not
for the six million, but was a word for me
and for many others. I was:
a survivor.

If that odd space following the first line's colon is meant to
signal the poet's discretion, it is not enough. A poet who has just
outraged the memory of a dead girl ought to have more qualms
about dragging in the Holocaust. To call herself a survivor be-
littles six million dead. The dead have their vengeance: the
adolescent sorrows of Sharon Olds do not compare with the
suffering of the raped girl, the murdered Jews.

Despondent mother, alcoholic father, drug-addicted sister—
family history should not be victim of such diminishment. Olds
is a sly judge of dramatic effect (her effects are her affect): the
images yoking blood to beauty create an economy of violence
where one horror can only be succeeded, or exceeded, by an-
other. Olds's life, the life that ought to be driven to violence,
remains distant and abstract. The images are the evasion.

Such violence is a form of sentiment, a sentiment confirmed
in poems for her children:

In the dreamy silence after bath,
hot in the milk-white towel, my son
announces that I will not love him when I'm dead.
. . . .
I do not tell him

> I'm damned if I won't love him after I'm
> dead, necessity after all being
> the mother of invention.
>
> ("The Mother")

This mistakes mawkishness for ferocity. Lost in stormy passion, she does not consider her implications. "I lay asleep under you," she writes, "still and dark as uninhabited / countryside":

> The inhabitants of my body began to
> get up in the dark, pack, and move.
>
> All night, hordes of people
> in heavy clothes moved south in me
> carrying houses on their backs, sacks of
> seed, children by the hand, under
> a sky like smoke.
>
> ("First Night")

From lungs to liver. From liver to pancreas. The transports of sex deserve less ludicrous expression. Or consider: "the blood on his penis and balls and thighs / sticky as fruit juice."

Olds is much too shy about using her poetic intelligence. Her similes rarely have Sylvia Plath's scary fastidiousness; the vivid perceptions ("the jets / float like shark along runways," "the hooks jerking / like upholstery needles through the gills") are lost in the bloodbath. The reader is tempted not to finish so many poems of violence and schmaltz (Olds is poetry's last chance to produce a romance novelist), and yet occasionally a last line will blossom into something unnamed, and unexpected.

The confessional poets talked their lives to death (late Berryman, late Sexton), but failure must be rediscovered by any poet of extremity. Olds's violent scenes discourage artistic shape—that lack of restraint makes Anne Sexton's poems inferior to Sylvia Plath's, though the pressures that drove them were equally evident, equally fierce, and equally fatal. Olds's poems don't yet have the emotional presence that would torture these lines to life—when she talks of killing, she doesn't sound dangerous at all. Her poems are more dangerous in what they leave unsaid.

Katha Pollitt

Olds rudely enjambs her headlong style; Katha Pollitt has better manners. Respectful of line breaks, her teleutons—almost always nouns or verbs at phrase end—hanker for solidity and completeness, an anchor in every line. Such a style is soothing as the slow rocking of a ship:

> That longing you have to be invisible,
> transparent as glass, thin air—
> that is what moves you certain times to tears
> watching the evening fill with city lights
> and the long dusty summer avenues
> rise weightless through the air
> and tremble like constellations in a sky
> so deep and clear you are your one desire,
> *Oh, let me be that blue . . .*
>
> ("Blue Window")

The self-addressed and banal phrases wash up against their breakwaters—*air, tears, lights, avenues*—and soon the apartment "grows strange with shadows, as though under water." The central tension in *Antarctic Traveller,* this shrewdly titled first book, is between what Pollitt so obviously is and what she cannot (or should not?) be. The landscapes she dreams on are obviously composed; only rarely is the longing violent enough for her to place herself within them. The poet, back at her desk, shyly discloses how far she is willing to go—only as far as, say, the library.

> What does the sea want, my clothes, my keys, my face?
> This is the mind's Sargasso,
> expansive as Kansas flatlands, the big dead place.
>
> The weeds stir, they make promises. I'm light as a shell.
> Immobile, the sea bottom
> glints at my emptiness with ship's tackle, jewels,
>
> railway tickets, photographs.
>
> ("In Horse Latitudes")

The strange is utterly domestic here, as if the sea bottom were a messy dresser drawer. The "mind's Sargasso" is a seascape not seen but imagined (a scholarly footnote explains the "horse latitudes").* This sea is not entered but entertained.

When Pollitt goes so far as to give herself to persona—and a mind entranced by history must be so tempted, despite its diffidence—she manages this breakdown of decorum by removing dangers to an aged narrator's recollection ("Of the Scythians") or by taming them with anachronism ("Penelope Writes"). Her Penelope is a repressed and angry housewife: "For years / I've sat at the window, those men at the kitchen table." What a homely, modern scene for Odysseus to return to!

Some of Pollitt's most lavishly overgrown poems, owing as much to Erica Jong as to Neruda or Wilbur, are paeans to vegetables:

> Like a dark foghorn in the yellow kitchen
> we imagine the eggplant's
> melancholy bass
> booming its pompous operatic sorrows
> a prince down on his luck
> preserving among peasants
> an air of dignified, impenetrable gloom
> or Boris, dying,
> booming, *I still am Tsar.*

("Eggplant")

The exuberant invention almost distracts from the dangling modifier. This craving for metamorphosis and yet suspicion of it can come only from someone committed to a fantasy world not superior or inferior but equal to the real one. Pollitt has a love of visual art (the central section of her book meditates on five Japanese paintings) that enforces the distance between observer and observed, real and ideal. Unlike Olds, who ruthlessly usurps the role of survivor, Pollitt approaches survival obliquely, through

---

*Or not so scholarly. Her explanation, that there becalmed sailors pushed horses overboard to lighten their ships, is the least plausible if most popularly printed of five I've seen advanced. Horses were, after all, valuable cargo. If they were deep-sixed, it was because water and fodder ran low. A duller possibility is that, entering the Sargasso Sea, sailors had worked off their advanced pay (called "dead horse").

the "you" that, in a poet of such self-reflective capacity, is often the "I." The only "you" is the one addressed in the mirror.

To the degree she understates herself she overstates her fictions. In poem after poem Pollitt seems too easy on herself, failing to question her romances (with images, not people—of lovers we hear almost nothing at all), allowing the most errant fable to pass for poetic truth (she loves maudlin exaggeration: "They danced on the rug and its errors blazed like stars"). There's something relentlessly cheery about her; she's as exhausting as a hostess hurrying guests through immaculate parlors, a Jackie Kennedy on an endless White House tour.

When the poet admits the distance her images impose, her art is of a higher order altogether—not because she is suddenly aware of language as evasion, but because the poem admits her evasions to herself.

> Well, what's wrong with that? Nothing, except
> really you don't believe wrinkles mean character
> and know it's an ominous note
> that the Indian skirts flapping on the sidewalk racks
> last summer looked so gay you wanted them all
> but now are marked clearer than price tags: not for you.
> Oh, what were you doing, why weren't you paying attention
> that piercingly blue day, not a cloud in the sky,
> when suddenly "choices"
> ceased to mean "infinite possibilities"
> and became instead "deciding what to do without"?
>
> ("Turning Thirty")

The jaunty self-mockery contains a note of resignation and despair.

Pollitt is more aware of contemporary social life than almost any of her peers—these pages are full of Roland Barthes, Design Research pillows, Baryshnikov, and the walnut tortes of Manhattan restaurants. The best poems dip below that glossy social surface and bring up rhyme both elegant and true.

> Let love go down to disarray,
> they sipped their water peaceably
> and nibbled the seed in their spoonsize manger

for all the world small citizens
still of that practical, prosperous land
where the towns sleep safe in the Emperor's hand
and fields yield fruit and women sons
and red means wealth and never danger
and even the thief hung up by his thumbs
bares black snaggle teeth with a sort of pride
to demonstrate for the watching crowd
to what swift grief all folly comes.

("Chinese Finches")

Pollitt is a poet who *believes* that folly comes to grief. Forget the agony of the thief (that's the rictus of pain, not pride). The qualities she takes as virtues, "reticence, calm, clarity of mind," are not crippling in someone so taken by the visual, made vertiginous by vegetables. Her reticence is her most attractive asset, most available in rhymes she has yet to exploit fully:

Those speckled trout we glimpsed in a pool last year
you'd take for an image of love: it too should be
graceful, elusive, tacit, moving surely
among half-lights of mingled dim and clear,
forced to no course, of no fixed residence,
its only end its own swift elegance.
What would you say
if you saw what I saw the other day:
that pool heat-choked and fevered where sick blue
bubbled green scum and blistered water lily?
A white like a rolled-back eye or fish's belly
I thought I saw far out—but doubtless you
prefer to think our trout had left together
to seek a place with less inclement weather.

("Two Fish")

The rhymes temper, a little too cozily, that horror of vision, the eye that suddenly sees too much. If those controlled emotions ever did break out, there would be a different picture altogether—"the ego glinting at the heart of things."

Jorie Graham

Pollitt dallies with transformation; Jorie Graham markets it. In *Hybrids of Plants and of Ghosts,* it is her characteristic trope ("See,

/ transformation, or our love of it, / draws a pattern we can't see but own"), and to it she allies a rare passion for the abstract. Her insights are profoundly poetical, not logical; but they live on the remembered edge of philosophy:

The Way Things Work

is by admitting
or opening away.
This is the simplest form
of current: Blue
moving through blue;
blue through purple;
the objects of desire
opening upon themselves
without us;
the objects of faith.

Such lines are attractively ideal. Graham is a poet convinced that everything will come out right, that if she works her changes long enough, the solution will pop into place, as on a Rubik's Cube ("The way things work / is that eventually / something catches"). Entranced by relation, she is intensely aware of the relative properties of language:

I Was Taught Three

names for the tree facing my window
almost within reach, elastic

with squirrels, memory banks, homes.
Castagno took itself to heart, its pods

like urchins clung to where they landed
claiming every bit of shadow

at the hem. *Chassagne,* on windier days,
nervous in taffeta gowns,

whispering, on the verge of being
anarchic, though well bred.

And then *chestnut,* whipped pale and clean
by all the inner reservoirs

called upon to do their even share of work.

The girl taught three names for the tree finds different properties in each, and the object in none. Raised in Italy, educated at the Sorbonne, NYU, and Columbia, Graham experienced in some form the trilingual upbringing described by George Steiner in *After Babel.* It may have contributed to her existence in the abstract, since any particular is subject to the shifting allegiance of language.

Graham thinks before she feels (many poets feel before they think): her poems are dedicated to the triumph of verbal arrangements. In a poetry that does not require emotion, any obscurity may be less abstraction than a failure to clarify the affairs between particulars. She chooses a subject, rarely with any necessity, as long as it can be forced to poetic resonance ("as if grown upward / from the meaning of the thing itself"), and then composes elegant variations upon it. She takes, say, ambergris:

> *Ambergris*
>
> Because our skin is the full landscape, an ocean,
> we must be unforgettable or not at all.
>
> Squids that are never seen alive surface
> to follow the moonlight on the water—anything
>
> that flees so constantly must be desirable.

This may seem like inspired trifling, but Graham trusts that language that sounds good means well. The first two lines pretend to logical exaction ("Because . . . , / we must . . ."), but the terms of identity between skin and ocean are tantalizingly undefined and the terms of choice ("unforgettable or not at all") spuriously conclusive. The following assertion is equally unconvincing ("anything // that flees so constantly must be desirable"). Retreating soldiers, delinquent children, bank robbers (who may be "wanted" but are hardly desirable) are contrary instances. But Graham continues—assertions, after all, are meant to provoke:

> In doing so they run aground or are caught
>
> by their enemy the whale. Sometimes fishermen
> hang paper lanterns on the prows of skiffs

and row backwards towards land. It takes
such a long time to believe

in evidence.
Consider the broken moon over the waves,

the missing scent of moonlight
on salt water—eventually

pattern emerges. The giant squid
is rarely seen alive, but whalers often find it

dead in whales.

"It takes / such a long time to believe // in evidence." The existence of the giant squid was long disbelieved, but that hardly justifies a general rule from a limited application. Some evidence (eyewitness identification, for instance, which is nearly worthless) is believed all too readily. Pattern may emerge from disparate bits of evidence, though what pattern the "broken moon over the waves" or the "missing scent of moonlight" may create is mysterious:

> There
> it exudes the powerful fragrance,
> its spirits—*Joy, Fly by Night, Green
> Paradise*—always working towards
>
> what must become the finished. Ambergris, what
> was her name? it moves before me almost within reach—
>
> jasmine, lavender, bergamot, rose . . .

Here, where the poem trails off like memory, the complex of associations is resolved. The fleeing squid, drawn along by moonlight, end in the whale's belly, as the fleeting recollection of a woman, drawn by a fragrance (the "missing scent of moonlight" perhaps?), lodges finally in consciousness. The tenuous link is the ambergris, the morbid secretion of the whale's intestine used in perfume. Olfactory memory is so tenacious a chance whiff of perfume, from someone passing on a busy sidewalk, can recall the presence (if not quite, the poem seems to say, the name) of a woman who wore it years before—"we must be unforgettable or not at all." We do not exist, except by evidence of the senses—ours or other people's. It may take a long time, as in the case of the giant squid, to believe in evidence. From such elusive intertwinings most of Graham's poems are made. But wouldn't the poem lie more within comprehension if it mentioned that ambergris is secreted to coat the whale's intestine against the indigestible squid beaks? Graham's poems love their vagueness more than their arguments.

Graham is a poet of process more than completion, whose range is not the stanza or line but the sentence. Because her enjambment is dramatic, the length of her lines varies from one syllable to twenty-two. Delicately functional, her sentences are like Ashanti gold weights; but she puts down whatever associations, however tortured, occur to her ("the tree ... elastic // with ... memory banks," "whipped ... clean / by ... inner reservoirs," "landscape, an ocean").* Her poems whirl their gaseous energy into vacuum.

Graham *toys* with ideas. She takes one seriously for a line or two, until there's another to be taken up and discarded. She's never awed or frightened by them—her attitude is insouciant, as if every idea were as fascinating as an egg. Because she never takes alarm at what she has said, she never finds in ideas an absolute questioning of herself.

Half nature, half spirit, *Hybrids of Plants and of Ghosts* is aptly titled—the phrase is from Nietzsche. Again and again Graham returns to the outdoors and the seasons (not surprisingly for a poet in love with the transformed), drawing her lessons by a sort of naturalist's modernism. Her obscurity is too great a love of rhetoric—the implications of her most striking lines must be patiently reduced, pared away to some often humdrum application. "Syntax" begins, for example, "Every morning and every

---

*Perhaps someone can explain Graham's association of a musical chord (I rule out the geometric) with braided or twisted hair ("twisting my hair, a chord / interrupted," "braiding their hair ... into its perennial solution, // cut chord"). Though sounds (especially three or more tones sounded simultaneously) might be braided, is a braid a chord, even metaphorically? Or has Graham merely confused *chord* with *cord?* It is tempting to suspect her of a sublime spelling error; but because Douglas R. Hofstadter has explored the affiliations between music and twining (in *Gödel, Escher, Bach: An Eternal Golden Braid* [Basic Books, 1979]), I must appeal to the readers, or the poet, for clarification.

dusk like black leaves / the starlings cross, / a regular syntax on wings." But whatever "syntax" these starlings create, whether random accident or ideal order, the poet seems to mean only that the crossings are uniform or that they correspond to some internal logic. Such language does not radiate from meaning, or into meaning; but Graham loves nothing better than to begin with such a line, half-magical, half-obscure.

Other people rarely figure intimately in her work—she's skittish about herself, unsure what to leave said or silent. Stevens, after all, is her poetic mentor, the Sunday afternoon philosopher Stevens. She doesn't have his dryness or his gaudiness, and at times seems just one of his characters—the lady in the peignoir, perhaps. "Drawing Wildflowers," her ars poetica, is dedicated to things:

> I can chart the shading of the moment—tempting—though shading
> changes hands so rapidly.
> Yet should I draw it changing, making of the flower a kind of mind
>
> in process, tragic and animal, see how it is rendered unbelievable.
> I can make it carry *my* fatigue,
> or make it dying, the drawing becoming
> a drawing of air making flowerlike wrinkles of the afternoon,
>
> meticulous and scarred.

Such poems seem endlessly refreshing because they never actually get anywhere. Her composition is intuitive, her poems full of those repetitions the mind at speed produces to ease its way. Her images, like her strategies, are little xeroxes of one another:

> *Chassagne*, . . . / nervous in taffeta gowns
> Snap- // dragon . . . , / dress of the occasion
> the catalpa have dressed in their fringes
> The chicory . . . , / purple heads / like grass skirts
> the water / a skirt the world / is lifting
> this cinderella land is in full dress, . . . her gown / lifting
> the ocean / flashing her green garments
> frozen vines of bittersweet have their mantilla
> each reluctant hem of greenery

Nature's costume designer, Graham is preoccupied with metaphors of sewing and weaving:

> starlings keep trying / to thread the eyes / of steeples
> the first thaw / threaded the water / like a needle
> the pincushion bush
> the crickets weaving their briar between us
> this morning once again find // something more gathered and
> tucked
> two wintered maples overlap sufficiently / to weave a third
> how still the spirit really is that threads us
> moments in our lives which, threaded, give us heaven
> lives / being snatched up like dropped stitches
> shade in the weave of severe / sunlight

Only a poet of narrow genius could tend such a high proportion of metaphors in such a small area of experience (and there is another series of tropes on knots, another on fabric). Once the reader identifies her strategies, she loses her freshness. Because her meditations depend on spinning out associations, her closures have the bias of the artificial; they are only metaphors of closure: "eventually / something catches," "all that you cannot give away," "the spirit breaks from you and you remain," "if I break you are you mine?" "finding the way to lose it," "reaches beyond us / to complete / only itself," "if she isn't gone / she lives there still," "she got him after all," "We caught the ones that sang." Almost half the poems end with such a hollow flourish.

The abstract is the most appalling subject for poetry, but for Graham the abstract is a necessary order—the real world constitutes the evasion (as if the abstract were real and the real mere philosophy). There have been other poets whose ideas of order have required a poem based on the line-by-line excitement of intellectual rather than emotional energies—just as, theoretically, life might have been based on silicon rather than carbon. Cocooned in their mental world, these accomplished and startling poems reveal a life not so much unreachable as uninviting—the reader often seems superfluous to them.

The Eclipse of Style

Galway Kinnell

In many cultures the division of the primitive universe—earth and sky, sun and moon, light and dark—is the personified division of male and female, those opposites Plato considered halves of a common form. Galway Kinnell and Marge Piercy are not antagonists, but their poetry is infused with the lived oppositions of sex, of sexuality. They are the male and female body of our moment.

Entering middle age, Galway Kinnell has published less frequently, and signs of mortal wear-and-tear are intermittently apparent in *Mortal Acts, Mortal Words,* his first volume of new poems since *The Book of Nightmares* (1971). Turning inward from the violence of his earlier work, Kinnell is rooted by the past, by "a narrow bed / where a girl and a boy give themselves / into time, and memory." The weight of memory is more substantial as he ages, and memory wears the consolations of loss. In elegies for his mother and brother, remembrance gathers the broken world into his work:

> his beauty
> of feature wastreled down
> to chin and wattles, his eyes
> ratty, liver-lighted, he stands
> at the door, and we face each other, each of us
> suddenly knowing the lost brother.

Kinnell often sacrifices such substance for cheap tears. The alien presence of the world once called forth poems out of the dark (as in his well-known allegory "The Bear"). Now he has become a benign, dotty naturalist. The new poems drift into an enervated musing that approaches the sententiousness of Robert Penn Warren:

> The bud
> stands for all things,
> even for those things that don't flower,
> for everything flowers, from within, of self-blessing.

These poems impoverish the nature they would describe. The mere existence of blackberries or a gray heron, starfish or a farm scene, is never enough: for this poet, they must exalt a visionary truth. Such poems supplement the poet's fatigue with the plenitude of what can be seen, but the profundities are spurious, the revelations banal.

In scattered lines Kinnell still writes vigorously—he describes Adam and Eve eating the forbidden apple, "poisoning themselves / into the joy." A few lines later he utters a commonplace ("No one easily / survives love") as if it were very, very wise.

Marge Piercy

"I have written these poems to be useful," Marge Piercy once wrote, a statement still true of *The Moon Is Always Female,* her sixth book. *Use* derives from a Latin verb that also means "to experience," and Piercy takes her poetry almost entirely from the happenstance of her life, its subjects ranging from unmarried love to that fate of the amateur gardener, an overabundance of zucchini.

Her slightly figured prose (she would call it poetry) is marked with purpose, casual beauty sacrificed to the urgency of getting things said, translating the barrier between mind and moment. Her life has a message, and she takes her symbols in action, not confession. In "Season of Hard Wind":

> I would go on, like Scott who trudging alone
> saw another plodding beside him as he starved
> and froze, his double, his despair, his death.

Recalling a celebrated passage in *The Waste Land,* the lines show the power of a longing that reaches beyond itself. In such poems what might have been programmatic becomes personal. But the need to be of use drives Piercy back to platitude, to wooden feeling, to a poetry trapped by its purpose: "We drive / toward each other on expressways / without exits," "What a richly colored strong warm coat / is woven when love is the warp and work is the woof." The overheated metaphors are fatal to a poetry of good intentions, especially a poetry so close to the lax discursiveness of prose.

Piercy's message relies on simplicity: she blames men for the antiabortion movement without remembering the thousands of women aligned against her; she rails against modern medicine but mentions the laparoscopy that eased her menstruation. If her poetry is to progress beyond the pettiness of message or the piety of self-congratulation, she must remember that the moon is not always female—in Semitic mythology, it is often male.

A. R. Ammons

Ground, tree, stone, hill—our landscape is Anglo-Saxon; at least, our vocabulary for it is. On this land A. R. Ammons has imposed a Latinate diction, an abstract and almost scientific language that dramatizes the disjunction between man and world:

> so that the longest swell swells least; that
> is, its effects in immediate events are least perceptible,
> a pitch to white water rising say a millimeter more
>
> because of an old invisible presence.

For Ammons, sight transmits the world too richly ("sight's // silk almost draws us away"), yet this abundance must be taken on faith, for the luxuriance of his vision can be inferred only from the depth of his reaction—his is a prose of seeing. The concerns of the poems in *A Coast of Trees* shift from world to man, from object to eye.

Ammons's poetry begins in the nature of Frost but ends in the objects of Williams; in the work of both, the mind copes with its surrounds. For Ammons, a man's cancer is only a horrifying expression of natural ripeness:

> the flames of climbing vines are
> shedding out, falling back,
> stringing fire
> the brook almost blisters with
> cool equations among the fallen colors
> what is to become of us we know
> how are we to be taken by it or take it

These lines voice a crucial artistic dilemma—shall an artist be possessed by the world or shall he possess it? Shall he choose mystic transport or analytic shrewdness, emotion or mind? Ammons is a poet of contrast who wants to talk continuity, his philosophy more Whitman than Whitehead, his voice intimate yet curiously unrevealing. More than the poets he resembles, he favors an intellect that in ordering the imagination orders the world. Less than any poet of intellect does he care for form, and his rambling observations are faint from lack of dramatic shape. His better poems have almost always been his longest, which catch the loop and whirl of his thought. His shorter work, as here, is undistinguished. Its tenaciousness and tenuousness, its fits and starts, might be expressed in his own words: "in debris we make a holding as / insubstantial and permanent as mirage."

John Ashbery

To overcome the inertia of silence, John Ashbery has set himself a task—to compose fifty poems of four quatrains each. Now titled *Shadow Train,* the poems were originally called "lyrics"— the word was ironically employed. "Clearly the song will have to wait / Until the time when everything is serious," Ashbery declares, but just as clearly *clearly* is impatiently spoken and these domestic "lyrics" are offered in the meanwhile. Readers are by now familiar with his sparring idiom, his voracious appetite; "the dream, reversed, became // A swift nightmare of starlight on frozen puddles in some / Dread waste" may quickly be followed by

> That's why I quit and took up writing poetry instead.
> It's clean, it's relaxing, it doesn't squirt juice all over
> Something you were certain of a minute ago and now your own
>   face
> Is a stranger and no one can tell you it's true. Hey, stupid!

That mixture of the serious and the giddy, insight and myopia, recognizes that language does not come to terms with age and death, but is our failed defense against them. Ashbery's airy imaginings, the dizzy swerve of his conversation, are tempered by knowledge of death. Some unusual poems come between the froth of invention and the fear of knowledge.

> The voice of reason is heard for a hard, clear moment,
> Then falls still, if for no other reason than
> That the sheriff's deputies have suddenly coincided
> With a collective notion of romance, and the minute has
>   absconded.

The present volume is temperate for a poet who exploits the violence intrinsic to language, awaiting only one word in its improper place to provoke angers of meaning. The quatrains, no matter how prosaic, seem restrictive to such an expansive voice; but his continual invention makes Ashbery the most stimulating (and occasionally most irritating) of our poets. Few demand so daring a reader. Where the heart of most poems, if beating at all, lies within range of a reader's surgery, Ashbery's work is of another anatomy altogether.

Sleeping Forms

Modernism has not completely driven love from poetry, though no reader any longer expects the innocent raptures of Browning on Browning. So skeptical has poetry become that purity in love is now impermissible—it violates our modern faith in discontinuity and contingency. Each of the poets under review has attempted to acknowledge passion. If the acknowledgments are tortured, they mark the extremity of such a breach in poetic etiquette.

W. S. Merwin

The attenuated tercets of W. S. Merwin's new collection, *Finding the Islands,* are kissing cousins of haiku: "Cold August / mice roll / empty nutshells." These tercets—composed in dozens, composed singly—find their subjects first in the splendor of mountain and island, then in erotic contentment. The pointillist method presumes that to fix the orbiting particulars around an observer is to fix the observer.

These are observations of a pale romantic: "The colors look back at the trees / but the birds shut their eyes / thinking to see it all again." It's hard to imagine a purpose in the errant wavering of these tercets, a reason toward whose recovery the poem directs itself. The aimless movement seems derived only from aimless imagination, which perhaps adequately describes Merwin's work after the brilliant concentration of *The Moving Target* (1963), *The Lice* (1967), and *The Carrier of Ladders* (1970).

Though they possess none of the dramatic juxtapositions or mystery of haiku, the better poems appreciate the epiphanies of Imagism:

Sound of Rapids of Laramie River in Late August

White flowers among white stones
under white windy aspens
after night of moonlight and thoughts of snow

The worst are brutally cloying ("I want to be buried / under your heart / where I was born"), pretentious ("when I am away from you uncounted / clouds of fish are calling in the seas / and nobody hears them"), and solemnly banal ("As I grow older / the cities spread / over the earth"). Moonstruck and nature-mad, Merwin has starved his verse toward anorectic perfection. It is touching that someone is willing to write so badly, out of love.

James Dickey

Beneath James Dickey's *Puella* is a love not erotic but conjugal. Described in the dedication as a "girlhood, male-imagined," these dramatic monologues are spoken by his wife, Deborah, though they have none of the reminiscent exactness of such a bold act of ventriloquism, none of the recaptured quality of girlhood. As child and woman she speaks with the invented, grown-up imagery of an adult poet and in the clotted syntax and compound nouns of James Dickey:

> no heat-shadow   nowhere to be left
> Behind   time-sparks over the grass   sunrise
>
> From blade to blade splaying in muscle-light.

This is Gerard Manley Hopkins as Alice in Wonderland. *Puella* is relatively free of the self-congratulatory lyricism and vaunting ego that have disfigured Dickey's recent work. Some lines recall the fine, stringy intensity of his earlier poems: "The stalled tightening of distant fruit, the wasp's delaying / Uncontested spasm at the pane." Too often, however, the language twists itself into a Gordian knot, the private tongue of poets who were never children:

> Some distance
> Down, unfurl   sit loosed and hawking
> At me, as I am hurled and buried
> Out of you in midair,
> In hounded flame-outs stalling and renewing,
> Pale with chasm-sweat, through Chaos
> Set going by imaginative laws,
> One flawless seizure bringing on another,
> The search-and-destroy of creatures in the void.

It is sign of the poet's extenuation, the pure drive of his language almost beyond meaning, that this is simply a dancer speaking to her audience.

This trust that sound will carry the sense rather overwhelms, in a metaphysical and metaphorical grandeur almost as awful as Swinburne's, the homely domestic scenes—Deborah running with her sister, Deborah in a tree, or with a horse, or burning her doll. It has long been Dickey's gift to inflate the ordinary out of all proportion—what can one make of Deborah "Imagining Herself as the Environment"? Though that poem is an unexpectedly touching elegy for James Wright, Dickey never lets something be done that can be overdone.

Hayden Carruth

Hayden Carruth's long poem *The Sleeping Beauty* is also a work of connubial love, in which the poet has converted his wife to a figure of folklore, through whose dreaming mind pass the images of heroes and the voices of women. The women are raped, murdered, sold into submissiveness—they are the women whom heroes, or rather ideas of heroism, have failed. Into this structure the poet inserts his own often bitter, doomed experience ("he will die, like everyone, stupid and alone") and the harshly beautiful landscape of Vermont.

Neither the poet's voice nor the structure (124 fifteen-line "sonnets") quite forces the disparate images into a transcendent whole—or even transcendent parts. The invocation of heroes and women is repetitive rather than progressive, and the metaphorical movement—the sleeping beauty toward waking, the poem northward toward the aurora borealis—parallels no equal movement of subject. There are admirable passages, however— the most serious, the poet's memories of the madhouse:

> And inside there he suffered interrogation, torture
> When they wired his head to voltage and shocked him
> Deep into the abyss, so that when he woke
> He couldn't remember who he had been, and they did it
> Again and again, and he sighed,
> "Why? What have I done?" and usually they evaded
> The question, but sometimes they said,
> "Nothing, son, nothing at all—you're just unlucky."

Behind the poem's historical personae and respect for the troubadours lurks Ezra Pound; the jazzy colloquialism and intimations of madness and sex conceal the John Berryman of *The Dream Songs*. Indeed, these are "dream songs," where the deflations of Berryman ("And he stood at his window and shook his fist at a cloud. / It didn't help much. It helped a little") are more welcome than the Provençal romance of early Pound (" 'May my weakness / Somehow still swell in your ardors a little, unbidden' "). The poem succeeds, not when Carruth serves these masters least, but when he steals enough to make them his own.

Karol Wojtyla

Karol Wojtyla's love is not secular but spiritual. His *Collected Poems* have been translated into English because their author happens to be the pope. Even in his wooden translated English (not always that inferior to the other poets' English), Wojtyla suffers the sincerity and fever, the redolent depth of love. His love is for abstractions (Man, Church, God) rather than the physical—as the troubadours knew, the abstraction of love allows its purity. It allows an overpowering emotion embarrassing when ascribed to an earthly lover. So warily do we approach the form of love we call such a lover demonic.

Much of the ideal of romantic love derives, as Carruth recognizes, from the troubadours. They, in turn, thieved their concepts from the church. Unfortunately, little of the now ambiguous language of worship ("passion," "adoration") thickens the verse of Pope John Paul II. His fondness for moth-eaten metaphor and vague effusion gives much of his poetry a weary abstractedness that sounds like gimcrack Eliot:

> We stand in front of our past
> which closes and opens at the same time.
> Do not close the oneness of comings and goings
> with wilful abstraction:
> life throbbed and blood dripped from them.
> Return to each place where a man died; return to the place
> where he was born. The past is the time of birth, not of death.

On occasion, for a line or two, the verse is seized by language more exacting: in an elegy for a quarry worker, "How violently his time halted: the pointers on the low-voltage dials / jerked, then dropped to zero again." Such lines do not atone for the clichés of feeling surrounding them. Even when the subjects are biblical, the poet captures none of the Bible's hard-edged imagery, its appreciation for the homely detail of desert, of temple, of market. That failure cannot be wholly the fault of the translator. Readers of this book may not mind its defects as poetry— the worst poetry, when written by a pope, serves other purposes.

Chronicle of the Early Eighties

Edward Hirsch

It is an exhausted time for much American poetry, when even Romantic has become just romantic. To the romantic, the real is worse than unfaithful. It's ordinary. Edward Hirsch's *For the Sleepwalkers* is preoccupied with the absurd assertion ("It has taken centuries to discover // The heart is a pomegranate") and the overblown image ("The sun is going down tonight / like a wounded stag staggering through the brush"). His metamorphoses are rotten and oversweet:

> How two black boys stepping out of a carousel in the park
> Resemble a spotted horse working its way
> Out of a cold lake in the rain. And how
>
> A spotted horse shaking the water from its mane
> Resembles two young country girls dancing
> On a makeshift wooden stage at a county fair
>
> In rural Georgia. And how those two young girls
> Move with the special grace of Nigerian clowns.

The imagism quickly becomes arch romance, avoiding the world by prettifying it.

This poetry refuses to take life on its own terms—a gauze descends between word and world. The aversion is nowhere acknowledged, or used as in Stevens to philosophical effect, spoiling even Hirsch's momentary beauties. A poet shying from his reactions can flee into persona; and Hirsch at times becomes a waitress, a seamstress, an acrobat, even a buzzard. Only when he can be somebody else, and that somebody Rimbaud, can he accept the world's harshness. The famous dead come in for much poetic exploitation here—Nerval, Smart, Klee, Matisse, Rilke. A quarter of the poems are consumed by this odd cultural vampirism—the dead are bloodless husks for the poet's imaginings.

This possessive inhabiting of other lives may be the bizarre compensation of someone possessed, for many of Hirsch's poems are uncannily reminiscent of Norman Dubie's, copying his affectations and even his reckless fondness for exclamation points. Only a desperate intelligence could mimic another poet's voice so keenly.

Leslie Scalapino

The elegant design and printing of *Considering how exaggerated music is,* Leslie Scalapino's first full collection, cannot disguise the disturbing mental states her sequences record:

> Haven't I said that part of having intercourse
> with anyone, is loving them when they are weak,
> When they can't speak. When a woman, say, mews
> (while being flipped over on her belly by a man) i.e.
> if she utters some sound sort of like what a doll
> makes, when *it's* flipped forward. What I mean by this
> is: her eyelids, after flying open with her head
> flipped back, will drop shut when her head is forward.
> And in falsetto   (we might even say mawkishly),
> the woman's mouth makes a sound like the word Mama.

Her poems seem an inner dictation, an eccentric mental process precisely taken down. The strain is to find the forms such thinking fits. Her dramatic punctuation, for example, indicates pause by a long space ("By morning,   naturally,   I was sated"). One might in her work speak of strong and weak commas: it's like gauging the length of Emily Dickinson's dashes.

So dramatic a form does not guarantee drama. The anecdotes she rattles off drift away open-endedly and ominously, with a weird matter-of-factness. At times her work becomes a Kafka grotesque—she's attracted to people who think themselves insects, or their lovers seals, dogs, plants, or baboons. One sequence, "Instead of an Animal," observes suckling and sexual urges in children. Another, "In sequence," breathlessly recounts travels through India, Africa, and America. It is never the news but the nuance that matters, and she is more alert to the shadings of social commerce than anyone except Ashbery.

Scalapino's flaws are all indulgence—she's garrulous, monotonic, bewilderingly parenthetical. Her onrushing syntax can be confused and almost illiterate, however necessary for the passionate idiosyncrasy of her poetry. It is not how she writes but what she pays attention to that makes her dark, uncharted poems unlike anything now being written in America.

David Wojahn

Among W. H. Auden's choices as editor of the Yale Series of Younger Poets were John Ashbery, Adrienne Rich, W. S. Merwin, James Wright, and John Hollander. No other Yale editor has equalled his cool prescience. In recent years, under Stanley Kunitz and now Richard Hugo, the series has been conventional as cottage cheese. David Wojahn's *Icehouse Lights*, though more appealing than the selections of the past two years, is still shackled by current American fashion.

The tiresome use of personal life, American poetry's peculiar legacy from Lowell, Plath, and Berryman, should long ago have been proscribed. Wojahn's childhood was made for poetry, perhaps manufactured for it—crippled mother, alcoholic father, blind grandmother and grandfather. Yet whatever pain these circumstances caused—and he returns to them with a need to relive childhood—has turned pulpy and bathetic: "Since memory becomes revision, / like sentiment in foolish songs, / we smooth our pasts and loss / until they're simple." To do so is to betray them.

Wojahn's glum, moody, all too earnest reflectiveness accepts the failures of his parents and the stillbirth of his lover's child. In small towns and claustrophobic apartments, he displays his sensitivity like a scar. There's nothing venturous in his work, nothing to offend propriety; but his poems are finely organized and his images exotic:

> the noises we make to ourselves
> in the night, tired
> as the lovers in a Japanese print
> who've turned and wiped their genitals
> with the blue silk scarves
> they had stuffed in their mouths
> while coupling.

Such images never disconcert an imagination otherwise wrapped in silky recollections, one that so conveniently appropriates the famous dead (Delmore Schwartz, Cesare Pavese, Buddy Holly) or distorts elementary physics (it is hardly possible to know a star has died before the light stops reaching us).

Gjertrud Schnackenberg

The dead are a bullish issue on the stock exchange of American poetry. "How much can we remove from the dead / for our private, selfish use?" asks one poet. Not enough, one might reply, before turning to Gjertrud Schnackenberg's *Portraits and Elegies*. A series of poems for her dead father, a long poem on Darwin in old age, a sequence about the former inhabitants of an old house: her book is a book of the dead.

Schnackenberg's luxuriant mastery of pentameter and rhyme serves an intelligence without muddle, an imagination that draws nature into severe alignment—a planter's clock, a row-boat on a lake, the faint moon dipping behind hills, the fish lurking in the water weeds. Schnackenberg lets her grief yoke the pale moon, seen when nightfishing with her father, with the kitchen-clock moon marking time after his funeral. The nature she inhabits is not benign:

> On our hot porch, a snake unhinged his jaw,
> A toad half-swallowed in his fatal kiss,
>
> Twin heads and double tongue that cursed our door.
> Now apples black with frost cling to the bough,
> And all around this house the cold grass stirs
> And breathes that frog's blue sob, Oh take me now.

Her poems must regard—in nature, in art, anywhere—the deaths that will make her father's death bearable. The poise and confidence of these formal images rival the glassy brilliance of Hecht and Wilbur. One would not expect a poet so bound by family and marriage to be conscious of history, though her father was a historian. She honors him by succeeding him, trying to solve in poetry the histories death leaves unanswered. Of the Bayeux tapestry:

> now the centuries of grease
> And smoke that stained it, and the blind white moth
> And grinning worm that spiraled through the cloth,
> Say death alone makes life a masterpiece.
>
> There William of Normandy remounts his horse
> A fourth time, four times desperate to drive
> Off rumors of his death. His sword is drawn,
> He swivels and lifts his visor up and roars,
> *Look at me well! For I am still alive!*
> Your glasses, lying on the desk, look on.

The dead are here bound to a living world. Such supremely rational poetry, the long sentences taking the measure of a thought and pacing it out, faces the secret horrors of the self without flinching, stares down sorrow before accepting it. If Schnackenberg is the most traditional of these poets, immune to fashion and the documentary impulse, she also cuts deepest. The clean lines of her style will be a lasting addition to our poetry. There was no better first book in America last year.

Carolyn Forché

The muddy kinship between private lives and public affairs darkens Carolyn Forché's *The Country between Us*. The first poems derive from her months in El Salvador, and her eye is arrested by the ordinary ("the oldest women / shelling limas into black shawls") no less than the horrifying:

> A boy soldier in the bone-hot sun works his knife
> to peel the face from a dead man
>
> and hang it from the branch of a tree
> flowering with such faces.

Too many political poems are written from moral innocence, as if the poets had been bred from textbooks. Forché's weathered irony—toward the pretensions of a twenty-year-old poet, for instance—sounds a more distrustful note.

Unfortunately, despite her reverence for the political, her poetry is trapped by current expectations. Poets now begin as autobiographers, and much poetry exists only as a vehicle for inner reflection and outer confession. Forché's attempt to make personal the horrors witnessed too often emphasizes herself at their expense. She's all too self-conscious of her role as a poet ("To my country I ship poetry instead / of bread, so I cut through nothing"), trading in symbols that haven't any of the coercion of events ("while birds and warmer weather / are forever moving north, / the cries of those who vanish / might take years to get here"). Her mystical strain turns blood into the blood of poetry. When a colonel dumps a bag of human ears on a table:

> Something for your poetry, no? he said. Some of the ears on the floor caught this scrap of his voice. Some of the ears on the floor were pressed to the ground.

The story is so grim she has cast it in prose, but the virtues of prose cannot save so poetic an ending.

Forché's work relies on sensibility, though she hasn't learned a language that will take reaction deeper than sensibility. When she tries to be poignant she is merely pretentious—"We have, each of us, nothing. / We will give it to each other." This is not to minimize what she has done. She has dragged into American poetry a subject too often considered alien to it. Her prose account of El Salvador, published in the *American Poetry Review,* is more terrifying and moving than poetry. Forché is better angry than elegiac—elegy encourages discursiveness and anger epigram. It might once have been the other way round, but now our tempers are short and our postmortems long.

Sandra McPherson

In previous books Sandra McPherson celebrated and even flaunted the domestic. *Patron Happiness,* her fourth, is more intimately autobiographical, though the intimacy may be accident, not change in philosophy. Adopted at birth, she recently confronted her biological mother; a few new poems explore her tentative gestures toward this stranger. The discovery turns back on herself, on the woman born not Sandra McPherson but Helen Todd. She says to "Helen": "I was not born. Only you were."

These unresolved relations vanish into nature. McPherson remains a gorgeous impressionist, whose inventions are a kind of rapture. She finds in nature what most poets cannot—an adequate imagination. It is not merely her metaphors that redeem the ordinary, though their gaudiness is raw as revelation—"Terns flash here, four dolled-up stilts in a pool, / Dozens of godwits a thick golden hem on the bay." Rather, such beauty restores to her, as beauty should, a sense of dangerous possibility. Whether implicated in a near drowning at a motel pool or in a mud cure at "The Spa of the Posthumous," nature retains its dangers even when tamed, its therapies even when marketed.

> The pre-Divinity majors I once knew
> Have all become gods by now.
> Their wives were always goddesses.
> But you and I were trained by weeds and boulders,
> Graduating to a part of nature.

McPherson is a painter whose real talent is painting rocks, not the picnickers or murderers lounging beside them. Her ironies do not let her forget that, though encounters with the manmade are the real desecrations, they are the world, like that of the adopted child, in which she must live.

Jon Anderson

As a title, *The Milky Way* has an unpleasant ambiguity, since Jon Anderson's recent poems have gorged on milky emotion. In any book of collected poems the new work may be betrayed by the old. Anderson's early poetry progressed from the excruciatingly self-absorbed *Looking for Jonathan* (1968) (the title alone should warn off the reader) to *In Sepia* (1974), which welcomed, not just the possibility of judgment outside the self, but a reflective capacity that could render the world as more than the alienation of particulars. In its economy of emotion and handling of abstract matter, that book was morally richer than the work of almost any of his peers.

> But if all our losses are a form of death,
> A mirror in which we see ourselves advance,

I believe in its terrible, empty reflection,
Its progress from judgment toward compassion.

The first lines have been revised to read "But if all our losses are a mirror / In which we see ourselves advance"—a gain in rhetorical efficiency at the subtle cost of resonance.

Anderson lapses into a sentimental regard in the presence of good. In "Lives of the Saints," he attempts to beatify Mozart, Clare, Tolstoy, Mandelstam, Rembrandt, Klee—as if their suffering were a *martyrdom* to art or idea. He has a point, but it's the wrong point about artistic suffering. The pain of artists, even in the service of their art, is not special. It is good to have his early books collected here, but they chart a life that after six or eight years of upheaval has settled into the blandness of compassion.

Jorie Graham

Jorie Graham's first book, *Hybrids of Plants and of Ghosts* (1980), was a frenzy of invention, bewilderingly and floridly abstract, produced by an imagination that might easily have burnt itself out. The calms of her second book lack her intransigent energy, her wild images startled into flight. *Erosion* in this context could have been dangerously symbolic:

> The tide
> is always pulsing upward, inland, into the river's rapid
> argument, pushing
> with its insistent tragic waves—the living echo,
> says my book, of some great storm far out at sea, too far
> to be recalled by us
> but transferred
> whole onto this shore by waves, so that erosion
> is its very face.

Where her personality was once drained by verbal ingenuity, the erosion of ingenuity has left Graham concerned with outward relations that manifest inward ones. The natural world serves the complications of philosophy. In poem after poem, the world is perceived through an intellect of sensuous natural images: a snake catching flies, bottom fish "driving their bodies through the mud," a water strider laying its gold eggs only "on feathers // dropped by passing birds / or on the underside / of a bird's tail / before it wakens and / flies off."

The ancient walls and richly embroidered culture of Italy, where Graham was raised, offset the uncivil landscapes of New York City and rural America. It is in isolation that Graham casts now into nature, now into philosophy, for some human contact and appraisal—her titles range from "Reading Plato" and "In What Manner the Body is United with the Soule" to "Wanting a Child." For Graham, poetry is still a mental construct, a declension of mind; the secret subject she veers from is loneliness. Even when her forms are truncated or her arguments impromptu and unsatisfying, her most exquisite poems maintain a tension between real and ideal that drives them past the surface of mental life and deeper than anything in her earlier work.

Amy Clampitt

Amy Clampitt is the most refreshing new American poet in many years; indeed, she is one of the few poets of major ambition and major talent now writing in America. After the bland prose that characterized American verse during the seventies, there has been a sudden lurch toward form in first books by Gjertrud Schnackenberg, Brad Leithauser, Katha Pollitt, and now Clampitt.

Like a number of other poets under review here, Clampitt is entranced by natural phenomena; where Jorie Graham uses nature to complement mind and Sandra McPherson emotion, Clampitt is simply engulfed by it. She has that love of pure description, like Stevens in "Sea Surface Full of Clouds" or Bishop in "Florida," that turns the physical world into an imaginative act.

> Where at low tide the rocks, like the
> back of an old sheepdog or spaniel, are
> rugg'd with wet seaweed, the cove
> embays a pavement of ocean, at times
> wrinkling like tinfoil, at others
> all isinglass flakes, or sun-pounded
> gritty glitter of mica; or hanging
> intact, a curtain wall just frescoed
> indigo, so immense a hue, a blue

                    of such majesty it can't be looked at,
                    at whose apex there pulses, even
                    in daylight, a lighthouse, light-
                    pierced like a needle's eye.

She does not adhere to form so much as strew her poems with
an array of metrical and musical devices all too little employed
lately in American poetry—and not with such offhand cheer,
such mischievous delight in the possibilities of language, since
the deaths of Marianne Moore and Elizabeth Bishop.

Clampitt might be a schoolteacher—the scrupulous field-
guide notes at the end of the volume encourage that
impression—but she takes so much pleasure in her subject that
one learns more by her example than her examinations. Just
when she begins to seem a poet of only the sweetest tempera-
ment, however, she confides a darkness beyond self-knowledge,
a loss that cannot be purged by either language or grief.

Like all ravenous imaginations, Clampitt's can make poetry
out of almost anything: water trickling down subway steps, Bee-
thoven's Opus 111, the sea mouse, or the disadvantages of cen-
tral heating. *The Kingfisher* at times seems a vast sampler, its fifty
poems a variety of stitches that still do not compass her gifts.
Clampitt rules an unruly crowd of moods and dictions, and her
range extends from elegy to satire. She has the timing of a
comedian and the poise of an actress, yet her poems remain
intimate, unassuming, often playfully detached. That easy tone
can disguise hard lessons.

                    Would Prometheus, cursing on his rock
                    as he considered fire, the smuggled gem
                    inside the weed stem, and the excesses
                    since his protracted punishment began,

                    have cursed the ocean's copious antidote,
                    its lapping, cold, incessant undulance
                    plowed to shards by wheeling porpoises,
                    hydrogen-cum-oxygen fanned up in mimicries

                    of hard carbon, diamond of purest water,
                    the unforbidden element crosscut by fire,
                    its breakup the absolving smile of rainbows?

These long sentences suspended on meter, this copious and even frivolous vocabulary, challenge what they borrow, transform what they steal. In the history of American poetry, a number of other poets have come late to a first book—Frost at thirty-nine, Stevens at forty-three. Clampitt, whose poems only began to appear five years ago, is in her early fifties.* There has never been anyone quite like her.

---

*Clampitt did not divulge her birth date until years later—she was actually sixty-three when *The Kingfisher* was published.

Auden's Images

Like so many elements of his practice, Auden's imagery deserves a book, though both his attitude and his compulsion might be more honored by an encyclopedia. Those whose tastes force a division between his poems early and late, or between the English Wystan and the American Auden, respond to a difference of which the image is necessarily a part. One may prefer early Auden for his tropes and later Auden for his mind without suggesting that the mind earlier or the images later were commonplace or insubstantial. In the early poems, however, the images are conspicuous for the ideas they enact; in the later they support or merely uphold what the mind wishes to call attention to, leading actors reduced to pages and footmen, if not footnotes.[1]

Auden's verse is distinctively mechanical; its very facility is the stain of calculation. Poem after poem, the lines are bodied forth with the effusive cleverness of the schoolboy or the sour enthusiasm of the don; but these are masks more than true manners—a coldness underlies them. The lines spew forth as if utterly interchangeable, one image for another, one rhyme for another, like the moralizing couplets of Shakespeare's sonnets.[2] It would not be surprising if either poet found in his agility a kind of disgrace; the honesties and warmth we impute to their poems may have been alien to their makers. Auden's early preoccupation with machinery was incarnate in the stamping dies that minted his images. He seems less a craftsman, at home with his leather belt and bench, than the owner of a vast factory, less Fabergé than Henry Ford.

Consider the list. The list may derive from a precision, even a prissiness, that must tyrannize in order to suggest ("Moraine, pot, oxbow, glint, sink, crater, piedmont, dimple") or from an inventive faculty that cannot suffer the *bon mot* when *bons mots* will do ("when any world is to be wrecked, / Blown up, burnt down, cracked open, / Felled, sawn in two, hacked through, torn apart"). There is something faintly comic in the seriousness of a list, an inadequacy of language only over-adequacy will satisfy.[3]

Auden's habits were cumulative, not integrative; he did not develop the Shakespearean instinct for shuffling through metaphors like cards. If his imagination was clerkly, it had to account for experience in such emphases as the list allowed. By its very accumulation the list may rummage through human acquisition ("under the eaves, in bulging boxes, / Hats, veils, ribbons, galoshes, programs, letters / Wait unworshipped"). It may scrupulously articulate a progression ("A word, a laugh, a footstep, a truck's outcry") that would otherwise require a street of extras or an army of adjectives. At best a list's elements exist in delicate tension ("The roads, the illegitimates, the goats," "Yes-man, the bar-companion, the easily-duped"); at worst they collapse into a ragbag of meter ("an important decision made on a lake, / An illness, a beard, Arabia found in a bed, / Nanny defeated, Money," "Nocturnal trivia, torts and dramas, / Wrecks, arrivals, rose-bushes, armies, / Leopards and laughs"). The list may become so long it strangles its own purpose; it may become merely a listing, its coordinates uncoordinated. One cannot escape, however, the playfulness and utter willfulness of a world arranged by threes and fours: "The physician, bridegroom and incendiary," "The dog, the lady with parcels, and the boy," "dandruff, night-starvation, or B.O.," "motor-bikes, photography, and whales," "Orchid, swan, and Caesar," "drains, bananas, bicycles, and tin," "sunsets, passion, God, and Keats," "The septic East, a war, new flowers and new dresses."

The list has large ambitions, but its means are small and additive, even addictive. It is as old as the *Iliad,* or older; internal evidence argues that Homer's catalogue of ships was filched from an earlier poem. Auden could make and later disown a poem ("Spain 1937") from a sequence of lists, a catalogue of catalogues. The list, however, is subject to its inner limitations, its stutter. It can contribute to dramatic action, but cannot normally be that action. By its nature it stalls, interrupts, prepares instead of provokes. The action and ambition must be elsewhere. The list serves as a locus of attention; and everywhere in his work Auden relied on technique or typography to supply similar loci, forces at work outside argument.

Our language was impoverished when typographical practice ceased to employ the capital as a common mark of emphasis, restricting it, like some *grande dame* of etiquette, largely to *proper* nouns, *proper* names. Auden's fondness for the Augustan Age may have hinted at the force of capitalizing his notions, of moving, as he writes in an early poem, "From the alone to the Alone." The capitals do not merely isolate and aggrandize; they have a personifying rigor, and therefore claim as their parent not Pope but Langland.

The character of Auden's abstractions only mirrors—in the way that a repressed don once through the Looking-Glass becomes a mad, triumphant logician—the abstraction of his characters. Wrath and Gluttony and Greed totter forth like Wonderland's pack of cards: "Wrath who has learnt every trick of guerrilla warfare, / The shamming dead, the night-raid, the feinted retreat," then "Gluttony living alone, austerer than us, / Big simple Greed." They are neither so human they can clothe themselves completely in allegory nor so inhuman they lack a rudimentary psychology or anatomy. Theirs is a world of shadow actions; and if they often partake only ironically of the world of being, it is because they are often occupied only ironically in that world. Their importance is exemplary, and they are introduced so their heads may decorate the gates of the palace, if we take meaning to be palatial and not circumstantial—that is, an action toward which actions are directed, not an accident of action (as Auden well knew, form calls forth its accidents, and we allow ourselves later to call inevitable what arrived by chance).

Most imaginations are habitual; they repeat their successes until they are failures. The implacable oddness that becomes a style (as a beauty may become an occasion, or a Beauty an Occasion) easily deteriorates into the tic of nervous affliction. When the capital letters have become a plague, noun infects noun until almost all are in danger of catching it. One may distinguish, however, between those nouns representing some political or social tendency (the Social Beast, Hobbesian Man, an Age of Care, My Personal City, The Unpolitical, The Hidden Law), psychological archetype (the Shadow, the Quest Perilous, the Not-Alone, the Naughty One), mere abstraction (Death, Success, Wrong, Duality, Law, Dread), and various cartographic and historical entitlements (the Battle of Whispers, Cape Consumption, the Tosspot Seas, the Sneerers' Ball, the glum Reptilian Empire), though each category, and especially the last, bleeds into others.

Through the thirties, Auden increased his tolerance for capitals until they became an addiction and finally a mannerism. It startles at first to come across "gaga Falsehood" or "Beauty scratching miserably for food"; but soon all of Auden's nouns willy-nilly became candidates for apotheosis, whether it was the "Lost People" or merely "Real Estate." This is not to minimize the effect of Auden's capitals. There is a great difference between saying "To go elsewhere" and "To go Elsewhere." The first emphasizes the leaving, the second the arriving, and arriving at a place so firmly Other it is not marked on any map. The first has a departure, the second a destination. *Another Time* (1940), Auden's first book after leaving England, fixes the border where he exiled himself in the neutral country of literature, though from its safe estates he allowed himself to issue bulletins on the battles evaded. It is a book made up of capitals as well as literary capitalists: Auden's pre-Christian pantheon of Housman, Lear, Rimbaud, Melville, Pascal, Voltaire, Arnold, Yeats, and Freud, with artistic nods toward Orpheus, The Novelist, Old Masters, and The Composer.

The ennoblement of nouns had effect only when practiced discretely. If all common nouns are in danger of becoming lords, where will the commoners be to make the lords *feel* like lords? Like all kings, Auden played favorites, elevating one noun through revision only to lower another: "Lords of limit" became "Lords of Limit," the "Lost People" the "lost people." An occasional countervailing tendency, in one who (like One) "numbers each particle / by its Proper Name," reduced proper names to improper ones. Time and usage can rub Plato to "a platonic pash," Descartes to "a cartesian doubt," but Auden's attempt to gain acceptance and accession for his terms (and the capitals assume an act of recognition by the reader) went further, to "the raging herod of the will," "kantian conscience," "De-narcissus-ized en- / -during excrement,"[4] "some mallarmesque / syllabic fog," and even "How grahamgreeneish!" Capital letters can of course appear without escort, either masking an identity at a historical costume party ("N died [to be replaced by S] // And took T's job," where the figures are Napoleon, Stalin and Tamburlaine), or enforcing an anonymity ("Conductor X, that over-rated bore," "Director Y," "Z the Designer").

The personifying tendency elsewhere supports the inhuman

world's appropriation of the human, whether it is signaled by adjective ("the griping fern," "the faithful roses") or, more usually, dramatized with Auden's blithe air of inappropriateness: "The stone is content / With a formal anger," "The roads are so careless, the rivers so rude," "snap / Verdicts of sharks," "The disconsolate clocks are crying together." For Auden the pathetic fallacy never existed. Though many of these inventions are ambiguously light in intention and dangerously comic in effect, like those crying clocks, they create a world of social expression where the psyche projects its emotion upon objects it cannot govern, objects that seem to possess perverse wills and desires. Auden's device admits what many poets have trouble denying— that the world acts as if rivers knew no etiquette and sharks sat in judgment (they are particularly suited to snap judgments).

Abstractions own the landscape in Auden, and have private provinces and duchies in recognition of their status. Their stewardship is guaranteed by the deed of *of;* the resulting metaphors create a panorama of incongruous and monumental geography: "the valley of regret," "the dykes of our content," "Your map of desolation," "the haphazard alleys of the neighbours' pity," "The green Bohemia of that myth." More rarely, the house and grounds furnish a domestic topography: "the sudden mansion / Of any joy," "the tower of a stammer," "the staircase of events," "the poky nursery of the brain." Even the animal or human world may contribute its possessions: "what worm of guilt," "The hot rampageous horses of my will," "the huge wild beast of the Unexpected."

It may not seem, given Auden's icy fecundity, to make much difference whether the stammer is a tower or a tor, desolation a map or a millrace; but their eccentricity must be bound the more firmly into the poem if they are not to seem mere ornament. The "map of desolation" is something to be folded by a man under a tree, "the tower of a stammer" not merely where someone is "prisoned," but a feature mimicking the throat or neck. When events are a staircase they can be climbed (and they occur one at a time, and in order); the brain when a "poky nursery" contains the dreads and desires of infancy. Such associations may be weak, as Auden may be weak; but the intention to anchor the metaphors, even or especially when they are employed for distraction, implies that Auden did not want his devices to seem merely devices, that their presence was meant to support the order of the poem.

It would be superfluous to say so, except that Auden was often by choice a frivolous and shallow poet. His devices, repeated with easy negligence, came year by year to seem less the master's touch than the apprentice's ungainly mimicry. His descent into light verse in the midthirties produced some of his master-pieces, but the effect of such masterpieces seems to have been an inability ever to recover the unself-conscious and direct qual-ity of his earlier poems, those which for many readers make Auden Auden. It could be argued that Auden was unable to sustain the manner of his early poems and had to cast about for compelling or comfortable alternatives; he was always a poet for comfort, and his late manner (or his late manner, then his later manner, then his last manner) behind the trappings and obsta-cles of form grew progressively cozy. Few would want to sacrifice the sharpest inventions of his light verse, early or late; they revived a form much sneered at. The ponderous overreaction of his poems of the late thirties and early forties, however, and the frivolousness increasingly woven into serious poems, *could* be blamed on the discovery that one could be serious by being shallow (some of Auden's later poems discovered the reverse).

The tendency to dramatize abstraction is often a special if striking use of Auden's favorite device, the vignette. To a great extent, Auden used image as archetype, divorced of the particu-lars that would specify or subdue it. His nouns, for example, are often features separated from landscape, existing more in the textbook than in any local topography ("Wind shakes the tree; the mountains darken"). Whatever realm the nouns derive from, they are isolated from actual circumstance, as if chosen from some Platonic catalogue, issued quarterly. Auden's images are essentially mental; his objects have passed through the recti-fying and distorting machinery of the imagination, if indeed they did not wholly originate there. They've been imagined before they've been seen. Auden's world was essentially color-less, and distant scholarship may quarrel over whether this was a social judgment or the result of color blindness (it may have been mere distaste, or distaste concealing an ignorance—"I've absolutely no use for colour," the young "Hugh Weston" said to Christopher Isherwood).[5]

The vignette contrived the social life Auden found necessary but not sufficient. If his poems were about life, they were about the life of mind; his vignettes exemplify life without overrepresenting it. Their minor dramas reduced the compass of the world to the limits of one action. Existing mostly at the edge of the frame, they are mentioned only to be ignored, like Bruegel's Icarus. In "Musée des Beaux Arts," Auden's great poem on margins, Icarus fatally plunges into the sea, ignored by the minor actors elsewhere in the painting, actors who under other circumstances might be similarly and fatally ignored (as, in another poem, "The sinister tall-hatted botanist stoops at the spring / With his insignificant phial, and looses / The plague on the ignorant town").

Such vignettes frequently have no effect on the course of the poem and constitute dramas half-glimpsed, stories half-told.[6] The human condition exists in them, or through them, but it is the condition of that condition to be hurrying elsewhere. They offer a suggestiveness forever shorn of resolution: "the blond boy / Bites eagerly into the shining / Apple," "A little crowd smash up a shop," "But the poor fat old banker in the sun-parlor car / Has no one to love him except his cigar," "The mad gymmistress, made to resign, / Can pinch no more."

Auden was fond of the double epithet or composite adjective, itself often a condensed or compressed vignette: "The shepherd-killing thunderstorm," "the jaw-dropped / Mildewed mob," "the bowel-loosening / nasal war cry," "an Emperor's / baldachined and nightly-redamselled couch." Elsewhere these adjectives are shards of simile, memories of metaphor: "cloud-soft hand," "the dry-as-bone / Night of the soul," "she joins girl's-ear lakes / to bird's-foot deltas." Such hyphenated compression reads as desperation, an attempt to forge the new from the scrap of the commonplace or stale. Auden's devices frequently have a similar desperation at center, an anxiety that the plain statement will prove too homely. The vocabulary of the *Oxford English Dictionary,* which in the final books became a menace, could not always hide the retailing of secondhand ideas.[7]

The vignette could deteriorate into delirious absurdity: "the river jumps over the mountain / And the salmon sing in the street," "When the mountains swim away with slow calm strokes," "A burning village scampered down a lane," or, in less cartographic mood, "The tables and chairs say suitable prayers," "In pelagic meadows / The plankton open their parachutes." Many of these moments represent the impossible or sublimely ridiculous, but Auden could easily become the lackey of his charms. It is not that tables and chairs play out their neuroses as atheists, but that such foolery could register as a nervous flight from seriousness.

The rhetorical device with which Auden is most associated is the simile. The special ironic and idiosyncratic type he patented was, though present early in his poetry, largely confined to half a decade, 1936–1941. Auden's characteristic similes depend on incongruity, proceeding from the oddly apposite to the severely unlikely, from the apprehensible to the absurd. Unlike similes that are almost wholly a dislocation of the visual (like those of the British poets of the early eighties called the Martian school), Auden's work darker and more indirect associations. There is almost never in his poems the breathtaking rightness that attends the perfect simile elsewhere (or the Martian similes, misleading the reader the better to provide a subsequent *Aha!* of surprise—they are poetry's answer to Capability Brown). Auden's similes exploit a suspicion that the comparison cannot possibly be apt; to make it so, the reader is forced to the leap of faith a *discordia concors* occasions.

In early poems, Auden's similes often let context inform their effects: "Here a scrum breaks up like a bomb" depends on the previous line, "War is declared there, here a treaty signed"; "Do thoughts grow like feathers" on "What's in your mind, my dove." Others have an ominous visual aptitude, less exact than eerie: "gradual ruin spreading like a stain," "fallen bicycles like huddled corpses." Later the terms seem increasingly improbable: "Who pursued understanding with patience like a sex," "Your breath's like luggage," "easy as a vow."

Vows are rarely easy, either to make or to keep, and context gives little comfort: "Climbing with you was easy as a vow; / We reached the top not hungry in the least." This may support "Climbing with you was easy as making a vow is easy," or "as this particular vow was easy," or "Climbing with you was as easy as making a vow to do so." It may even propose that as long as the climbing was *only* a vow to do so, it was easy. Depending on preference, the reader may have to posit a world where vows are made as effortlessly as broken, where the climb (and this climb has sexual significance) was no more morally or physically corrupting than a New Year's resolution forgotten on New Year's Day. The intricate reasoning such similes demand results from limiting the comparison to something not immediately apparent, or at least something that cannot immediately be assented to.

At times it is easier to acquiesce to the incongruity than attempt to untangle it. The similes of greatest compression, however, are often the most satisfying; they arrive like a small electric shock: "remote as plants," "the sea / Calm as a clock," "he frowned like thunder," "The winter holds them like the Opera," "Kept tears like dirty postcards in a drawer," "Anxiety / Receives them like a grand hotel." Because they distort an object to favor a resemblance, such similes are highly artificial, often dependent on suppressed metaphor; they emphasize rather than explain. Not simply subservient to appearance or other intrinsic qualities, they recast their objects: "wears a stammer like a decoration," if a stammer is something to be worn; "nude and calm like a great door," if a door is a Venus de Milo. Auden invented the simile that altered what it advertised. The affect, as so often, easily became affectation; Auden is equally responsible for "the poets exploding like bombs," "hairless people / Who like a cereal have inherited these valleys," and "As a trombone the clerk will bravely / Go oompah-oompah to his minor grave." The last is preceded by "Metaphor bamboozles the most oppressed."

The simile has been considered a weak rhetorical device, whimperingly dependent on qualities, tiresomely explicating what metaphor would pounce on. Auden reclaimed the simile as a compressed vignette, an epic simile of dwarfish shape, dramatizing its objects without overwhelming them. Auden's tropes were still ruled by objects, but objects that adopted the sense of the simile. By such displacement new meaning was smuggled in; the simile was for Auden a form of order, not ornament.

There is no space here to consider those rhetorical imageries Auden handled well, even magnificently, but not oddly or unusually. His metaphors, for instance: "empires stiff in their brocaded glory," "Truth is convertible to kilowatts." Of them a chapter could be made, with perhaps a short note on unusual verbs ("that God or Nature will abrupt her earthly function," "Shall we ever become adulted," "dwellings / vacancied long ago," "I'll coffin you up") and the use of certain adjectives, like "crooked."

Auden's rhetorics are a kind of exhaustion, as if an infinitely complex calculating machine programmed to certain tolerances had churned out endless examples of a type. The repetition of means may explain why Auden so often changed his forms; his limitations were less evident when employed for constantly different ends. Yet these same limitations created an expectation gradually fulfilled. They may be what we mean by style: not what a poet does but what he cannot help but do. It is not attractive to think of genius as a residue, as what the author is least responsible for and may least value; but the images of Auden's poems order themselves into strategies that drive other strategies out. Auden's imagination found certain types of expression and certain subjects immensely congenial. His attachment to them reads less as possession than embrace.

II

Auden's imagery is a system, and a system coherent and controlled, though perhaps not at every level conscious. It gives a greater impression of unity, of the collaboration of many compulsions, than that of most poets—that is, it expresses an ur-story, a view of the world actual and ideal, yet one too idiosyncratic to command complete conviction from any reader. Auden's early poems are reports from a front not yet opened, a border that exists only by mental cartography. His images recur with such frequency he doesn't seem to have to seek for them. In later poems the imagery of this world was diffused, an old myth whose elements lingered long after belief had vanished.

The myth—the interior fiction that acts as myth—may be, perhaps has to be, unconscious. No intelligence would allow such coherence without troubling its terms; the simplicity, even simplemindedness, of an interior myth argues for its steady if unconscious bearing upon the art. Art often has a great and banal simplicity at center—it is the artist's elaboration that cloaks it in the earned genius of civilization. The earned genius, however, requires the rude simplicities.

The key line in early Auden is perhaps "For the game is in

progress which tends to become like a war." The poem is about love, but the game is played in earnest. Only through two qualifications is it allowed to become warlike—that it *tends* to become so (but need not), and that it tends to become *like* a war (not necessarily a war itself). Auden was not everywhere so hesitant to identify the combat around or within him. He could even joke about it:

> Lone scholars, sniping from the walls
> Of learned periodicals,
>   Our facts defend,
> Our intellectual marines,
> Landing in little magazines,
>   Capture a trend.

> ("Under Which Lyre")

Elsewhere, "From morning to night, flowers duel incessantly, / Color against color, in combats // Which they all win." Any sort of conflict (even the fight of the flowers) may be seen in terms of battle, but in Auden from the earliest poems the world is a battlefield where secret wars are being fought. These wars may be secret because fought within, or because others do not recognize they are fought without; in either case it is the poet's duty not merely to chronicle them but to enlist himself on the right side. Auden's twin gods of inner and outer are Freud and Marx; he appropriates the doctrines of both without fully converting to the religion of either.

Auden's early images were private and ingrown. They derived from the school world of his friends, their coded languages and pet names; later, as he traveled Europe and taught in boys' schools, they incorporated fragments from private life. Context offers no clue, and the reader may assume details are allegorical when they are merely personal (this is not the only form of Auden's obscurity). Early or late, Auden's images were forced from the personal toward the allegorical. The references may have been plain to Auden's circle, for the poems served as a public encoding of private thoughts, to be deciphered by those possessing the code (even if the property of Auden alone). It is not clear how much the world of the public school promised these early fantasies of Us versus Them, but the fantasy soon matured into a lumpish *Weltanschauung:* "the mouse we banished yesterday / Is an enraged rhinoceros today."

Auden declared in "September 1, 1939" (the date of Hitler's invasion of Poland) that "I and the public know / What all schoolchildren learn, / Those to whom evil is done / Do evil in return." Children acquit themselves in their fantasies of war; boys' magazines are as guilty of encouragement as newspapers. Auden's vision was weighted by the casual murders and strict codes of the Icelandic sagas, to which by birth and temperament he was early attracted (he was later to translate them). His home theater, crossing the betrayal and violence of sagas with the schoolboy world, fashioned a landscape where belief matched blood, where idea was an irritant.[8] Not many schoolboys are Auden, but more than a few have made lives from martial fantasies.

There is a war, then, or two sides engaged in an unnamed and unnameable conflict. The sides become countries, the countries share a border. The border is the seductive symbol of Auden's early poems. Psychological, political, or sexual, it is the demarcation between sides as well as an intersection of them. It may occur variously as a frontier, a partition, a boundary, or merely a line: "Before you reach the frontier you are caught," "Love by ambition / Of definition / Suffers partition," "where two fears intersect," "not stopped at / Borders by guards," "The frontier of my Person." The war may be imminent or declared: "morning's levelled gun," "Are you aware what weapon you are loading," "Soldiers who swarm in the pubs in their pretty clothes," "Europe's frozen soldiery." As the thirties progressed, the imaginary wars became actual ones, and it was either Auden's gift to have seen where the violence tended or his fate to have his private system made public.

The landscape of these countries in tension may be strewn with barbed wire and guarded by sentries: "The barbed wire runs through the abolished City," "Sentries against inner and outer," "The seasons stood like guards." The world is a system of entrances, exits, passages, bridges, gates: "Control of the passes was, he saw, the key," "passports expire and ports are watched," "Through gates that will not relatch / And doors marked *Private.*" These are places of transition and danger, where to be safe one has to change identity. The lovers standing on the bridge between the properties of the ambassador and the admiral seem safe in the power and glory of their love, unaffected by past wars and lost provinces. This is illusory:

> Nothing your strength, your skill, could do
> Can alter their embrace
> Or dispersuade the Furies who
> At the appointed place
> With claw and dreadful brow
> Wait for them now.
>
> ("Deftly, admiral, cast your fly")

The war can be reduced to (or can destroy) love and lovers, and the frontier may be only the boundary of the self. There is always an enemy: "Orders are given to the enemy for a time," "the visible enemy," "It is an enemy that sighs for you" (this last is followed by "Love has one wish and that is, not to be"). The air is full of conspiracy and revolution: "Waiting with bombs of conspiracy / In arm-pit secrecy," "Shooting and barricade in street" (such imagery could again become literal after the sixties—"young radicals plotting / to blow up a building"). The world is populated by strangers ("A stranger to strangers over undried sea," "Look, stranger, at this island now"), assassins ("Patrolling the gardens to keep assassins away"), and spies ("Our hopes were set still on the spies' career," "As agents their importance quickly ceased"). There is some personal identification with these silent, secretive actors, especially the spy, who because of his intellect, his homosexuality, or his political beliefs must always inhabit a country whose intentions are hostile. Like the exile, he may never be able to affect the decision of his false world or communicate to a true one ("They ignored his wires. / The bridges were unbuilt and trouble coming").

I need not linger on the talk of missions, groups (both bad and good—"The gross behaviour of a group," "the erudite committee"), secrets, and escapes. The imagery is markedly juvenile, embarrassing in its schoolyard vision, as what conflict is not? Auden's "charade" *Paid on Both Sides* (in *Poems* [1930]) and his "English study" *The Orators* (1932) (the country-house and public-school origins of *charade* and *study* summon up only a little less quickly the respective false and ironic associations) detail the psychology of the group at war, a group strikingly like, when it is not in fact, a bunch of cynical or idealistic schoolboys. Soldiers are often not far removed from the schoolyard; the playing fields of Eton, not Oxford, determine the course of battle. The wars fought through such imagery are distant from the Battle of the Marne or the Bulge, from Ypres or St. Lô. The men who win these paper battles are later not crippled veterans holding the Croix de Guerre; they are heroes: "the would-be hero of the soul," "The hero was as daring as they thought him."

Shorn of identifying characteristics, such nouns are already halfway to allegory. It is hard to know how much the mental landscape thereby impoverishes the physical one, yet the virtue of Auden's work is precisely its removal from the physical world and its substitution of a mental and moral discipline. Auden used the horrors of war, at least early in his career, to veer into his private imagery; and he tended to drop from his canon poems, like "Spain 1937" and "September 1, 1939," that too overtly or too ambivalently practiced politics. This first realm of his imagery, war and conflict, could stand under the statue of St. Freud (the old gods become the new religion's saints) for something as private and dangerous as love. Under the statue of St. Marx, it became a class war: "the retired and rich / From the french windows of their sheltered mansions," "isolated like the very rich"; these against "The ugly and the poor," "the poor in their fireless lodgings."

The second realm of Auden's imagery lies in nature, pastoral as counterimage to politics. The transitional image is that of the map, which may, depending on its use and its user, be benign or malignant: "Gone from the map the shore where childhood played," "like a lying map," "generals are already poring over maps," "might-be maps of might-have-been campaigns."

Auden's topography is northern. Born in York to a family claiming Icelandic descent (later he equivocally noted, "First I write *I was born in York;* then, *I was born in New York*"), he could not shirk the northern temperament or the landscape that created it.[9] Except when travel turned the world sideways (and Auden's first travel book was *Letters from Iceland* [1937], as northern as one might wish to be), his maps illustrate a hard, glacial topography: "From scars where kestrels hover," "the issue of steam from a cleft," "Curlews on kettle moraines," "lonely on fell as chat, / By pot-holed becks," "Tundras intense and irresponsive seas."

The landscape is cold and forbidding, everywhere hemmed in by glaciers: "glaciers calving," "The ice-sheet moving down," "the encroaching glaciers of despair." Circumstances determine its employment, but the glacier is an image ominously available, even as a chilling domestic feature ("The glacier knocks in the cupboard" has harsh associations of famine, though it might have proved an amusing description of a refrigerator).

Auden's landscapes are not otherwise exceptional, though their elements may be drawn into psychology or emotion: "In strangled orchards," "most desires end up in stinking ponds," "The mental mountains and the psychic creeks," "the deathless minerals looked pleased." They can have, on the other hand, a true pastoral air, free of mental fetters though at times mystical and strange: "Hearing the frogs exhaling from the pond," "lush alluvial meadows," "And the great plains are for ever where the cold fish is hunted."

Nature has its borders and battles too, and the border Auden most insistently recognized was the sea. These adjoining scapes confront themselves in "The eager ridge, the steady sea," where the human nervousness of "eager" infiltrates the solid probity of "steady"—the line is remarkably unsteady in its reversal of roles. In Auden the sea may be "ignorant," "irresponsive," "corrosive," "easy," "untamed," or "calm as a clock." Ships are everywhere ("Luxury liners laden with souls," "Our navy sailed away and sank"), as well as sailors, and piers and quays ("Like a sea god the political orator lands at the pier," "a primitive, unsheltered quay").

The seas, caves, mountains, and valleys of Auden's disengaged geography might have come from topographical glossaries, not any individual observation. From the isolation of islands to the mystery of caves, landscape plays out its dramas in psychological terms. One generic domain, the features could support any myth, generate any tale. "Bucolics" is Auden's symbolic reading of some of them (Winds, Woods, Mountains, Lakes, Islands, Plains, Streams), though it omits the caves that were his personal emblem (in "Thanksgiving for a Habitat" there is both a Cave of Making and a Cave of Nakedness, and Isherwood recalled how "Hugh Weston" liked even in summer to sleep under a heavy pile of blankets, coats, and rugs).[10] Auden's imagination worked from the literature toward the world, not vice versa.

The flora and fauna of Auden's poems are ghostly presences. In "Posthumous Letter to Gilbert White" he asks, rhetorically, "How many // birds and plants can I spot?" His answer: "At most two dozen." Would he have known a kestrel if he saw one, or a scar? Was geography, like nature, just a series of resonant syllables? His poems flicker with starlings, swallows, sparrows, ravens, rooks, chaffinches, and even sedge-warblers, the common birds of English field and hedgerow. His mammals range further, but he has a decided partiality for lions, tigers, and bears, leaving the reader to wonder whether he had visited them in a zoo (or was merely recollecting *The Wizard of Oz*). His odd animals and common birds, in their vague reality, might populate fairy tales. Auden's idea of nature may be said to begin with the harsh geography of northern maps and end with the chittering and growls of the *Märchen*.

Fairy tales are the link to the dreads of psychology and the heroism of the quest, to the third realm of Auden's imagery, the social order. The folktales represent the past shorn of history, the static past replaced and repeated each generation. They are the blood of the people, sometimes even the mind, and their settings the haunted domains of nature: "That calm enchanted wood," "Wiltshire's witching countryside." Their inhabitants are, in great number, ogres ("met the ogre and were turned to stone," "The cocky little ogre"), dragons ("This is the dragon's day," "A sterile dragon lingered to a natural death"), witches ("the roaring oven / Of a witch's heart"), giants ("The giantess shuffles nearer"), dwarfs ("a sobbing dwarf / Whom giants served only as they pleased"), and elves and fairies.

These are the figures the hero may meet on his quest. The quest for Auden is often the journey of spiritual discovery; it informs not only the sonnet sequence titled "The Quest," but also *The Ascent of F6* (1936) and *The Age of Anxiety* (1947). In later poems the hero has been tamed, become merely a traveler; in Auden the observer, whether he is the airman (many poems exploit the overview) or the sightseer, accepts a necessary distance from events in order to judge them. The traveler mirrors the exile, who cannot choose his banishment and cannot return, or the spy, who journeys for others and journeys in danger and disguise.

The fairy-tale characters symbolize for Auden the undirected psychic possibility the modern age would cleanse itself of. In many examples they struggle for their lives; they are threatened as well as threatening. It is a fairy tale even to find them in serious poetry, from which they were driven a century or two ago. There is no hope of restoring their position; in Auden they make no last stand. They are anachronisms the modern world has ground down to ghosts ("Where ghost has haunted," "any influential ghost") or mere shadows ("chased by their shadows," "my ignorant shadow"). The *Märchen* echo through other sorts of mystical or supernatural imagery, including cards ("All the dreaded cards foretell"), mirrors ("a land of mirrors," "your echo and your mirror"), and even such ancient ceremonial occasions as marriage ("Bride and victim to a ghost," "deep in clear lake / The lolling bridegroom, beautiful, there").

The mystical can easily be domesticated, turning up as an Agatha Christie mystery: "Where the body of his happiness was first discovered," "Who left a hairpin in the room?" The countryside in Auden is not even as up-to-date as in Christie. It seems to mediate between the primordial terrors of the woods and the modern contrivances of the city, and to exist in some post-medieval and pre–World War I limbo. There are knights and ladies ("chaste Milady awoke blushing," "The Knight at some lone cross-roads of his quest"), nobility of various sorts ("A Grand Duke's glass coach," "Lord Lobcock," "evil Count ffoulkes"), and servants who might have groused in any century. Peasants lurk about: "Tight-fisted as a peasant," "the pious peasant's only son." The house and grounds, however, are the real landscape: "One sold all his manors to fight," "country houses at the end of drives," "country houses long before the slump." The home, if not the castle, was the center of Auden's security; homes and apartments (and even the lowly bed-sitting room) have an importance only hinted by his sequence "Thanksgiving for a Habitat."

Country life centers for Auden in manor and village, modern life in the city—a city chillingly indifferent to the human. The city models the disfigured social order, where police must maintain a presence ("lights burn late at police stations," "in the policed unlucky city"). Auden's ideal may be the "Just City," the "Good Place," or the "Just Society"; but these are all versions of the "Great Utopia" distant from the "dark disordered city" (a metaphor, in fact, for Matthew Arnold; Randall Jarrell noted how often Auden turned people into landscape).[11] Auden's city is drearier and more depressing than Eliot's London, because he recognized more thoroughly the city's hopelessness. In Auden's city, his generic city (even when writing of, say, Macao, he found it hard not to make it a symbol), the lives are thwarted or pathetic: "timid bar-flies boast aloud," "old men in hall-ways / Tapping their barometers." Even the city plan shows only "Each great coercive avenue and square."

The elements of modern life, absurd enough when singled out for praise ("Read *The New Yorker,* trust in God; / And take short views"), mark the absence of the spiritual, the soulless striving after material satisfactions: "I shall build myself a cathedral for home / With a vacuum cleaner in every room," "*Pamina* may a *Time* researcher be / To let *Tamino* take his Ph.D." Even learning must be associated with commerce, even the characters of *The Magic Flute* end up short of funds.

The two urban institutions beyond the petty ambitions of commerce and industry, though sometimes corrupted by them, are science and the church. Science is forward-looking: "In scrubbed laboratories research is hastened," "Nothing, says science, is impossible." It is so forward-looking, in fact, it may destroy us, whether with "Honeyman's N.P.C." or the hydrogen bomb ("unless at the nod / of some jittery commander // I be translated in a nano-second / to a c.c. of poisonous nothing / in a giga-death"). Auden's hopes for science are tempered by its tendency toward amoral knowledge; it creates the circumstances where "Quite soon computers may expel from the world / all but the top intelligent few." Science is anchored to "the virile bacillus" and images of disease: "the false journey really an illness," "germs besiege / The walled towns." The church, for later Auden irresistible, is earlier ridiculous, tied to outdated beliefs, offering (like the stone of Oxford) "a bland hymn of comfort." It can do nothing but abdicate: "The Pope may quit to join the Oxford Groupers," "The Pope's turned protestant at last." The Anglo-Catholic Auden might not have made such fun of Rome, but his faith tended to be personal and a little mystical even after his conversion, his respect reserved for Christian ideals, not idolatry. The hierarchy of the church always tended to be stuffed with fools: "my modern pieces shall be cheery / Like English bishops on the Quantum Theory," "Law, says the priest with a priestly look, / Expounding to an unpriestly people, / Law is the words in my priestly book."

If neither science nor religion can offer comfort, it is the fault of the modern world's worship of industry. Everywhere in Auden men are seen by their occupations. Though some men survive outside the middle-class social order—beggars and thieves, hermits and hangmen (especially hangmen—there are a score of references to hangmen and gallows)—the world is the province of the clerk and the banker, the judge and the stockbroker, the diplomat and the doctor. The stock characters are the predictable gestures of the commedia dell'arte. Stock characters may be expected to have stock passions, and every poem must reconcile its passion before it can presume upon its intellect; or so the early Auden seems to have thought until he migrated to America and accepted a citizenship in prose (where intellect may presume on passion and finally drive it out altogether). In Auden's world of action, a man is only what he does.

Industry ruins, and industry is a ruin. Auden's images, despite his striving to be au courant, tended to derive from the twenties and thirties, not the sixties. That he was fond of machines is well known. Though he wrote that as a child the moment came when he was forced to choose the brutal and efficient machines over the merely aesthetic ones,[12] still "In my Eden we have a few beam-engines, saddle-tank locomotives, overshot waterwheels and other beautiful pieces of obsolete machinery to play with," and, elsewhere, "Tramlines and slagheaps, pieces of machinery, / That was, and still is, my ideal scenery." That machinery has changed the world, Auden recognized. There are few examples to suggest he thought it had changed for the better.

There is a beauty in the juxtaposition of mechanical and natural, where "Smoke rises from factory in field," where "The dripping mill-wheel is again turning." But elsewhere, everywhere, the machinery is silent: "An industry already comatose, / Yet sparsely living," "The derelict lead-smelting mill," "Abandoned branch-lines," and the stark list:

Smokeless chimneys, damaged bridges, rotting wharves and choked canals,
Tramlines buckled, smashed trucks lying on their side across the rails;

Power-stations locked, deserted, since they drew the boiler fires;
Pylons fallen or subsiding, trailing dead high-tension wires;

Head-gears gaunt on grass-grown pit-banks, seams abandoned
    years ago.

                                        ("Get there if you can")

This is a country abandoned to and then ruined by industry, where there is "Equipment rusting in unweeded lanes." The collapsed economy produces images of general sterility and decay: "Hearing of harvests rotting in the valleys, / Seeing at end of street the barren mountains," "Through bankrupt countries where they mend the roads," "Conduits, ponds, canals, / Distressed with weeds." This economic dislocation, this overturn of the social order that extends through the natural one, returns us to the first realm of confusion and contention.

To consider his poetry this way makes Auden's private myth seem more a fairy tale than it is—but our private psychologies are often mere fairy tales (often more like fairy tales than the fairy tales). The realms of Auden's images have further complications, and I have no space to explore the psychological divisions of doubles, lying, and dreams, associated with both the secret wars and the world of mirrors; the telephone and post office, institutions of social connection allied to Auden's many references to gossip and rumor; the ever-present and slightly terrifying symbol of the clock; the influence of the classical world, particularly Greek gods and Roman polity; or the references to Eden or Adam and Eve. The grand tour of Auden's imagery has yet to be taken.

Auden's early images, however distanced from the world, however thoroughly calculated, seem derived from felt emotion, whether the experience is actual or not; the emotions may be cool, even chilly, but they are recognizably individual. The American Auden used and reused feeling that had hardened into prejudice. When his practices became habitual, they had nothing to feed on but themselves. The later career studies its icy depletions, a mere idea in one book labored out to a sequence in the next (sometimes, indeed, a grand one). The expansive and devouring poems on literary figures are reduced to the pathetic clerihews; the brief turns of wit that prefaced his books become the jottings or joggings (called "Shorts") that infested them. The late sequences are lovely; exhaustion can be a form of creation, but it is different from the danger of Auden's early work. Loneliness and isolation, the futility of action, and architectures of decay were the tenor of his imagery. He wrote his biography in the terms of technique.

In his late poetry, Auden's techniques rarely created an entity sufficiently larger than his effects to blind the reader, however temporarily, *to* those effects. One must like the late poems *for* their devices, *for* their repetition of familiar imagery. Increasingly one must respond to his poems as a mind, not a creature of feeling. Auden may have been the minor poet he saw himself to be, even the minor poet he eventually made himself; but compared to this sort of minor poet most poets may be forgiven for feeling minuscule. Auden may secretly have preferred that his facility be admired before his faculties. His devices have proved a wicked temptation, and he knew enough about sinners to wish perhaps to be sinned against. Even if readers one day forget the poems of high-browed civility; of ticklish, infantile genius; of Parnassian bonhomie (no one this century wrote *more* memorable poems, and almost no one wrote more *memorable* poems), no poet could use a certain type of list or simile, could employ certain images of industry or folktale, could capitalize an abstraction, without summoning up his name.

In Exile

Though their concerns be political or social, most poets are poets of landscape, identified by a place they are devoured by. Indeed, a coherence of scene is so customary, as if poetry were still subject to Aristotelian unities, that an international poet like Ted Hughes or Derek Walcott risks seeming disjoint by invoking landscapes of more than one country. The cultures of the Caribbean, Ireland, England, and America are tied historically by the British Empire, their poetry so mutually comprehensible that unity of place is as anachronistic as the stagecoach. The four cultures are nevertheless not one culture.

Derek Walcott

Midsummer, Derek Walcott's new sequence of fifty-four poems, is repetitive and rancid with language, a sourly glorious view of middle age and the end of middle age. Walcott is a writer of sumptuous elegance, who may perhaps be excused if he sometimes mistakes the elegance for passion. The landscape of one year, midsummer to midsummer, falls on sets from the Caribbean to Boston for a man now in exile at home and at home in exile; but he has become more sensibility than subject, a clutter of images roused to riot.

> Gold dung and urinous straw from the horse garages,
> click-clop of hooves sparking cold cobblestone.
> From bricked-in carriage yards, exhaling arches
> send the stale air of transcendental Boston—
> tasselled black hansoms trotting under elms,
> tilting their crops to the shade of Henry James.

Walcott has always been ravished by the visual: this book drowns in the one sense, calls in painters (Watteau, Cezanne, van Gogh, Pissarro, Gauguin) like policemen, and splashes one of the author's watercolors on the front cover ("light, in their view, was the best that time offered"). A notebook of this sort, and Robert Lowell's comes to mind, must be careful not to let the thrill of rapid notation, of catching each shift in the seasons' splendor, steal a sense of design and of warrant ("Midsummer bursts / out of its body, and its poems come unwarranted").

In the last decade Walcott has occasionally seemed confounded by his gifts. *Midsummer* shows the pressure and hurry, the repetitions and longueurs, of a book willed into existence; but the will is an inadequate goad to poetry, unless the poet is suffering a more interesting psychological disorder than middle age. Walcott's frequent, nervous invocations of the poetic act ("I cannot connect these lines with the lines in my face") seem empty acts of compulsion. Nevertheless, in poems whose designs outlast the determinations of the merely visual, he uses his aging to darken the assumption of these luxuriant images: that whatever is, is beautiful.

Seamus Heaney

Seamus Heaney's task in *Sweeney Astray* has been to recover for modern English the medieval Irish text of "Buile Suibhne," a legend in verse and prose. Sweeney, a headstrong king, is enraged at being sprinkled with holy water before battle; he spears a psalmist and almost murders St. Ronan. The bell around Ronan's neck stops the spear aimed at him; but in vengeance he calls down a curse, and Sweeney is condemned to wander the land mad and naked, a pitiable creature who lives in trees and can fly. Repetitions and contradictions reveal the rough transmission of the poem between the thirteenth century, the probable date of its oral composition, and the seventeenth, when it was finally written down. Such metamorphoses are no less maddening than Sweeney's, and Heaney admits that in one place he has been defeated by the text's complete obscurity.

Heaney's own poetry is redolent of the peat bogs; and his command of language at times animates the ancient legend, founded on the Battle of Magh Rath (Moira) in 637:

> At Moira my tribe was beaten,
> beetled, heckled, hammered down,
> like flax being scutched by these women.

Sweeney's wanderings around Ireland (the poem might be one of Ireland's first travelogues) provoke him to plaintive verse:

"Forever mendicant, / my rags all frayed and scanty, / high in the mountains / like a crazed, frost-bitten sentry." The language of the original does not often provide moments for Heaney's crisp and coarse inventions, and the quatrains are frequently undistinguished and embarrassing:

> The psalter that he grabbed and tore
> from me and cast into deep water—
> Christ brought it back without a spot.
> The psalter stayed immaculate.

Metrical and idiomatic clumsiness so infects the poetry (at one point Sweeney's wife exclaims, "My poor tormented lunatic! / When I see you like this it makes me sick"), it's a relief when the legend lapses into prose. *Sweeney Astray* is a labor of love, and like much love tells us about the laborer. The poem was composed for an audience that knew the landscapes these dry place-names mean to evoke, places that, as Heaney notes in his introduction, have fond meaning for him. Heaney has not been able to replace the music of the Irish original with an English equivalent; the rambling course of Sweeney's madness, though moving in its hopelessness, has finally little moral interest or point, except that it's wise not to go around throwing spears at saints.

Ted Hughes

The *River* that courses through Ted Hughes's new collection is the sum of many rivers carved from many landscapes. Hughes is a poet of almost elemental potency, and his work here has been possessed by the struggle between the implacable rush of water and the brute muscular salmon swimming against it. If Walcott is a painter, Hughes is a sculptor. The consonantal thud of his language ("The gouged patient sunk in her trough of coma") and the words thrown hard into new positions ("From a core-flash, from a thunder-silence / Inside the sun") are trying, not to exact from language a visual equivalent, but to capture the world's physical thrust and pummel, its rushy anger. The river reeks of renewal, is redolent of rebirth; but, even when celebrating its abundance, Hughes seeks the deaths beneath or beyond:

Summer wastes in the pools.
A sunken calendar unfurls,
Fruit ripening as the petals rot.

A holed-up gangster,
He dozes, his head on the same stone,
Gazing towards the skylight,
Waiting for time to run out on him.

This is the salmon, doomed after mating in its natal pool. The mathematics of its crippled mortality can be altered only by man's intercession. At a salmon hatchery, on the day before Christmas, the poet watches salmon milked of their eggs and sperm, the glut of life spilled into a kitchen bowl. To cast such a poem on such a day is grotesque and mawkish; but Hughes is always eager to over-prepare and over-determine, to let the last line of a poem labor an effect carefully achieved (English understatement is often anathema to English poets). The doomed mathematics of salmon has all too appropriate significance for such a carelessly prolific poet. It would be difficult to make a lyric of every landmark, a sonnet of every salmon.

Philip Levine

Philip Levine's landscape is subdued by machine and memory. From the factories of Detroit and the orange groves of California, the furnaces and railroad yards, the early deaths and lower-middle-class pallor, his work derives its urgency and grace. The verbal dramatics of the other poets reviewed here have been sacrificed to the plain speech that accents Levine's crucial vanity—his regard for his own humanity. The persona of a man's poems may be at variance with the man writing them; but Levine's partial recognition of that vanity comprehends his immersion in the madness and evil uselessness of life.

All night at the ice plant he had fed
the chute its silvery blocks, and then I
stacked cases of orange soda for the children
of Kentucky, one gray boxcar at a time

with always two more waiting. We were twenty
for such a short time and always in
the wrong clothes, crusted with dirt
and sweat. I think now we were never twenty.

He is tortured by hope and invigorated by despair. In these *Selected Poems* his concerns evolve from the peculiar formal poems of his first books (a man butchers an angel, a pig speaks on its way to the slaughterhouse—"I can smell / the blade that opens the hole / and the pudgy white fingers // that shake out the intestines / like a hankie") to the consolation and sorrow of family life and the political disasters of the Spanish Civil War—the one a compulsion to recall, the other a refusal to forget.

Though superficially more distant from daily affairs, the early poems spoke from a deeper and more discouraging psychology than the family dramas that followed. Levine's recent work has been more elusive, its narratives at times suppressed almost past understanding; his last book explored alternative lives—as a fraudulent train conductor, a pilot, a fox, or just a voice—as if his own life had been eviscerated. A worldly fatigue has long since entered his poetry, its monotone imposing a line lax to the point of prose, its rigor not language but spirit. That spirit in the face of hopelessness has made his poetry valuable. Though still subject to the warm tears of memory, Levine sees steadily and clearly the fate of children, "the foolishness of the world / they will try not to inherit." It is almost as if he believes poetry might be proof against fate.

In the Medieval Future

Science fiction is a version of pastoral, more dependent on Theocritus than space travel. Like pastoral, its simplicities are deceptive. The ease with which complex social ideas may be invited into simple characters has seduced many serious authors, most recently and disastrously Doris Lessing. In his epic poem *The New World,* Frederick Turner's misshapen ambition is to fuse science fiction with medieval romance, finding in the future the grim corruptions of the present and from those corruptions forging an idyll.

Four centuries from now, the Earth's oil and gas reserves, uranium deposits, and mineral resources have been exhausted. The world has been depopulated by emigration to distant planets and the slaughter of the middle class. The great nation-states of the twentieth century have been whirled into the vortex of history, the USSR collapsing into its ethnic groups, Japan into its company families, Europe into the catchment areas of its soccer teams. In the United States (called the Uess), the cities have become "Riots," lawless matriarchies feeding off the slave labor of the suburbs. Outside are only Mad Counties and Free Counties: the former are fundamentalist theocracies, constantly warring against the Jeffersonian democracies of the latter. It isn't hard to guess which estate Turner favors.

James George Quincy, the young Perceval of this tale, walks out of the madness of what remains of Manhattan, carrying his father's sword Adamant. He and his mother head through the Mad Counties of Vaniah (Pennsylvania) toward their home in the Free Counties of eastern Ahiah (Ohio), a land of milkweed and honey. It can be reached only through lines of battle, where armies of knights train lasers on each other:

> Meanwhile with a scream and a whoop
> the rockets rush from their tubes and converge in red cones
> on the tanks, strung out among the plodding foot soldiers.
> With cracks like lightning the ion paths are established
> that will guide the punching pulses of laser light into
> their targets; the valley floor leaps into detail and perspective

as bursts of actinic light like chrysanthemums flower
in series along the line of the road.

James joins the engagement and returns home a hero, prepared for a destiny of further battles, military and romantic.

The conventions are familiar; but, however ingenious the adaptation of American geography to epic mythology, an epic relies on the telling more than the tale. Like some poets and apparently all critics, Turner has a theory of prosody, though the practice has proved considerably more difficult than the preaching. The problem of the long poem in our century has been the fashioning of a verse line adequate to the classical diversity of incident and tone. When *The New World* is confined to the jungle of nature or the special effects of battle, the verse has the texture of visual attention, awful though it is as poetry. Given the poet's philosophical and literary ambitions, the prosody elsewhere produces a line indistinguishable from prose and therefore incapable of subtlety as a poetic medium. The poem's invocation implicitly announces the limit of invention:

> I sing of what it is to be a man and woman in our time.
> Wind of the spirit, I should have called upon you long ago
> but you would have me gasp, draw dust for breath,
> weep without tears, spoil the tale in its telling,
> wander an emigrant where no garden grows
> before you'd take me back into the bosom of your word.

This tormented mixture of crude histrionics and dime-novel romance ("draw dust for breath"!) is small challenge to "Arma virumque cano" or "Of man's first disobedience, and the fruit."

Turner's real interests are the ethics and social organization of his new world. After the first sweep of narrative, the poem stalls in long tracts of genealogy and the complete college education of the heroine. The weary lessons in future legal history, economy, religion, and art have the wooden suggestiveness of a sociology text:

> Government revenue
> consists in the equal contribution of all the voters
> and cannot fall short of expenditures. Every child
> gets an equal share of the budget for education

as a token current in any accredited school.
Health care follows the same kind of system.

Few poets can versify legal code. Epic (and science fiction) worlds are called into being by dramatic action—the drama offers the social detail its ragged necessity, illuminating a world of which narrative reveals only a part. Turner is so enamored of his fanciful contrivances, he cannot bear to leave any out. The elaborate caste system of the Free Counties, with its Kshatriya-Samurais (warriors), Shudras (farmers), Vaisyas (merchants), and Brahmins (priests), proves of little consequence. No one is inconvenienced by it; no battles are lost because of it.

James George Quincy wins his bride after surviving three ordeals; and there follow private grief, public grief, battles against dark forces, capture, escape, two years lost making his way home via the star colonies and "Calyforny," and various episodes of conflict and reversal before he can face for the final time his enemy, the Messiah of the Mad Counties. *The New World* thieves shamelessly from *Beowulf, Burnt Njal's Saga,* the *Odyssey,* the story of Abraham and Isaac, virtually the whole range of myth and romance. The borrowings are part of Turner's method, but here obligation is a form of contempt. Kingfish, the hero's black mentor, lives in the abandoned subway system beneath Manhattan— he is the Fisher King with his secret wound and James the Perceval who must ask the proper question. Kingfish's homely philosophy is rendered arcane by an accent not much employed since the casual racism of dialect novels:

> "Yo' done
> broke through de doors ob de edge ob de world
> an' now yo' want to know how yo' can love
> what yo' seen from outside. Ah got a question for you:
> Why not? Ain't dat a sucker?" "If the world is a game,"
> says James, "knowing that, how can I act
> with all the pitch and momentum of action, if life
> is merely illusion?"

This ludicrous clash of dictions, composed in utter sincerity, is a stray exhibit of the high comedy to which Turner's epic is subject.

The New World is only the old world, our own culture drawn and distorted. Science fiction ages gracelessly because its projections are helpless and automatic. Transient contemporary phenomena, not current so much as au courant, govern the social organizations of the future; a reader can everywhere trace today's concerns in tomorrow's guises: here feminism, there bioengineering, all to be outpaced by the next decade's headlines. Turner has the original theory that the mere imagining of this romance guarantees or at least influences a better future. The science fiction of the forties and fifties did not guarantee a better present, and there is little reason to suppose current science fiction will have much effect on whatever future we are allowed. Science fiction is wish fulfillment of the most nakedly adolescent sort, and to imagine it has serious cultural or literary consequence is to be a naked adolescent. Turner has created, not an epic that will "serve as an opening to a post-modern creative era," but a classic of camp literature.

In the Architecture of Absence

Vicki Hearne

Too much has been wormed from obsession for poetry to be solely the product of a healthy imagination. The biographies of modernism are exercises in the crabbed insufficiencies of private life, from Eliot's trusses and green makeup ("the colour of forced lily-of-the-valley") to Lowell's conviction while in a mental hospital that he was John Milton revising "Lycidas." The *Cantos,* the *Dream Songs,* the "sonnets" of Lowell's *Notebook:* these are one poem damned after another, the narrative impulse and even the thread of continuity thwarted by the longing to repeat and return, to become what the poem just became. These are the sequences of metastasis, replications in the disease of form that have as much to do with stasis as change, that are cancerous and brilliant.

Much of our poetry's neurosis has been formal, experience reduced or revised to fit the arbitrary structures the imagination demands. Such structures are not limited to sonnet or sestina, blank verse or dactylic hexameter. Even Pound's sprawling *Cantos* insist on a narrow range of formal gesture, the verse not free but foreseeable; compared to the liberating accretions of the *Divine Comedy,* their fussiness is constricting. Pound's obsessions were subject to their subjects as well; and few who have read the *Cantos* care to acquaint themselves further, or ever again, with the radical economics of Major Douglas. Formal obsessions are transparent; only in the inscrutable recurrence of idea does the pathological imagination grow interesting.

Vicki Hearne's first book, *Nervous Horses* (1980), was a fabulous jeu d'esprit whose poems repeatedly explored the history or habitation of the horse. From "Riding a Nervous Horse" to "Rebreaking Outlaw Horses in the Desert," from "The Metaphysical Horse" to "Daedalus Broods on the Equestrian Olympic Trials," equine ontology argued an imagination not only sufficient to its infatuation, but wholly defined by it. Whenever Hearne's poems deviated from her enthusiasms, her verse denied its passions. As she wrote in the book's final poem:

I have become cautious, but

Still I should speak of horses,
Emerging and shaped just so
In the inchoate tangle

Of our truths, how clarity
Sparks in the shift of their hooves.
                                        ("The Metaphysical Horse")

The title of her second book, *In the Absence of Horses,* is a shrewd
commentary on the content of the first by a poet who knows the
value of obsession. It is also a gesture calculated to mislead, since
her horses are never more present than when supposedly
absent—they are ghost images on a television screen, from a
station too remote to be more than interference. When the title
poem is reached halfway through the book, scarcely a horse hav-
ing trammeled its pages, absence is the argument for presence:

In the absence of horses
The Beloved will suffice
And will change on the brutal
Turns of the tongue, becoming
The Betrayer, betrayed, and
Hollow figure of fullness
For seventeen years until
At last lovers, abandoned

Again to their gazing are
Figures of knowledge, figures
Of action for which any
Steady emblem is enough.
                                    ("In the Absence of Horses")

Without horses, lover turns betrayer (and in betrayal of the
tongue the eye wants to change *gazing* to *grazing*). Horses gallop
through the remainder of the book as a reminder that art will
always recover the agents of its pleasure and that the strategy of
a book's order may be as artful as its title.

Hearne's second book is a more abstract exercise than her
first. Image has given way to idea; her style is less nervy than
nervous. She begins with the skittish presentation of hypotheti-
cals as if they were actuals: "So: we don't nestle weightless / In

each other's hearts! The soul, / Then, is a raptor." That is the standard procedure of metaphor, which exists less often as a clarification than as a clearing away of other possibility: the soul is x rather than a-w or y-z. Assertions must make their case by the accrual of particulars, or attend to the structures of thought, as in Stevens. Here assertions are marshaled with complacence. The consensual relations between author and reader have broken down, and the rhetorical beckonings ("So," "hearts!", "The soul, / Then," "and if," "Is that it?") are not evidence of an argument, only of sensibility. "Is" makes as many appearances as the comma.

Hearne's conjectures are so bereft of conviction, she sleepwalks through her poems, out on the thin ice of pure language:

> To pass over in silence
> Is to acknowledge logic,
> The necessity of form,
>
> The stunning curve of language,
> The curious way it seems
> To turn out that "love" means "need"
>
> Even in a lush garden.
>
> ("Passing over Your Virtues")

There is no lush garden here, much less a stunning curve of language. For a poet with passions so curious, the danger in a dry language and a dry logic is that they ask a rhetorical flourish to bring them to closure. After stanzas of self-denial, poem after poem rises to the vacuous sublime: "I begin / To speak of it all, to speak // For my impetuous skin," "This is why I fuss / Over the harmony I live with / Out hope of, why the song must go on,"* "we are / Ourselves after all, damaged, / Brutal, and speaking, brutal / And pure," "Hush up! Nothing sings but time / In the sizzle of embers," "Its significance of galaxies // Wak-

---

*The lack of a hyphen in the line break "with / Out" may be calculated, since it occurs twice in the book, or merely another sign of the volume's inadequate proofreading, which among other problems has left "It's" for "Its," "prophesy" for "prophecy," "winey" for "winy," "Brigher" for "Brighter," and "thiry" for "thirty."

ens us and God is born again." Such endings would make an end to any poem.

In *Nervous Horses* the severity of idea and grandeur of feeling existed in fruitful tension. Once an animal trainer, Hearne now teaches philosophy at Yale and is an essayist of distinction; but neither philosophy nor prose saves her from fatuous affirmations breathed in complete sincerity: "dance we must or / Lose our hearts to the bare truth // Unmourning physics with her / Knowledge of the dazzle of / Cosmic entropy displays," "Invoke what bright energies / You find here, breathe my name and / I'll breathe yours, into valleys," "Your eyes, ruined by calamaties [*sic*], / Jerk in the corners of bare chasms."

This is sentimental poetry of a curious sort. For all her talk of love and the sexual ("loins" is a favorite word), rarely has sexual passion seemed so chlorotic. Like many poets who have pondered the blank page too long, Hearne has found poetry a convenient figure for itself, and for everything else. Most poets are occasionally tempted to use as tropes the tropes of their craft—to make *simile* and *metaphor* and even *poem* the adequate words of an inadequate world. The ingenious critic may find every poem an *ars poetica,* but the ingenious poet doesn't need to make it so. Soon poems are everywhere: "a giant poem / Struggles, just there, in the ocean," "The rider prevents / The approach of poetry," "in the poem's / Flesh a grain of sand," "This poem of the only instinct," "that is beyond the poem now."

In a poet for whom saying is the crucial trope, it is odd how much is left unsaid, and odder how much is said over and over again, as if the repetition defined the art of poetry. These poems are speech acts in a double sense, and their duplicity is such that they can say without meaning far more often than they can mean without saying.

Mary Jo Salter

"We know how much we take on the faith / Of the tongue. Japan, for example," writes Hearne. Mary Jo Salter doesn't need to take Japan on faith, having lived there. One of the many attractions of her first book, *Henry Purcell in Japan,* is its view beyond the American horizon. Hers are not questions but answers of travel.

Mia cugina, with the black-olive eyes,
escorts me arm-in-arm through her church,
leads me from saint to saint in search
of the chapel where the Savior lies.
"Ah," she sighs, and pulls back the drape,
exposing Him rose-strewn, pink and yellow—
Easter colors. "*Non è bello?*"
she whispers, seeing my mouth agape.
His wounds look fresh, but it's not this sight
that shocks me so much as His man-made skin:
He's waxen, slick as a mannequin.

("For an Italian Cousin")

Had it been prepared by something beyond rhyme, *agape* might have admitted into its precincts the *agapé* so plainly lacking. The tourist's social ungainliness makes the more affecting her struggle to redeem herself, before her cousin as before the wax mannequin Christ: "Tempted to joke, I'm silenced by / the trusting expression on her face, / flushed with the light of this stained glass / where Christ is always about to die." Irreligious, Salter can flee only toward a faith in the grandeur religion engenders.

Salter's book again and again flies to acts of contrition, to religious acts in secular atmospheres. In a museum she comes across a facsimile chapel, its walls Sheetrock, not stone, where

it was difficult to feel sure
of a holy presence. But isn't God everywhere?

Or nowhere? In the cold light of reason
(above the stained glass, track-
lights one might find in a modern kitchen),
I thought of that blindered, overbearing knight.
I wouldn't have brought back his Crusades,
wouldn't confess to sins that don't
originate with me.
                    Yet knowing of my share,
and knowing I'd never happen, in my own
century, on a place better to look,
I pulled up a chair.

("Facsimile of a Chapel")

These are moments to which education is unequal, when the secular must pull up a chair before ancient altars.

Salter urges her poems toward such revelations, but begins them with an offhand, diminishing mien, as if all the world were a toy box, reminiscent of Elizabeth Bishop: "How disastrous it looks— / the rust washed into the rocks, / and the wrecked ship itself, picked clean. / It was 1911 / when the Evangeline beached here." How easily this echoes the cool pleasure-taking of Bishop's "White, crumbling ribs of marl protrude and glare / and the boats are dry, the pilings dry as matches." In Salter's work, however, that immanence is often religious, despite her disclaimers ("As it always does when I forget / I'm not really a Christian, my heart / flew to my knees"). The book's epigraph, after all, is from Herbert—"How should I praise Thee, Lord! how should my rhymes . . ." The tenor of her best work is essentially devotional.

The poems have a cheerful, self-correcting tone, full of rhetorical questions and emphases ("Just *how* did she come to be there. . . ?" one poem begins). Everywhere there are mocking or explanatory parentheses, stage whispers that render informal the formal motions of narrative: "('What did you suppose?')," "(since I'm writing *your* story)," "('French: 12th century')," "(I still wonder, / Did you stand up on your head?)," and "(your favorite: Earl Grey)" do not begin to suggest their variety or profusion.

The last parenthesis in the book—"(everything reminds of something else, / but nothing of what is not already here)"— describes their fever as well their limitation: they remind the reader of something else, something to be remarked on but nothing not already there. The parenthetical comment cannot be worked into the text; it is not even truly latent there—the text has no room for it, has been composed in a pace or a sequence of detail that forces its exclusion, or at least seclusion. The parenthesis withholds even as it releases, stands outside even as it stands inside.* The religious impulse in Salter's work similarly resists suppression; excluded, it still will voice its discontents. These contraries beneath the work's imperturbable silver plate, its occasional delicate (though not always perfect) filigree

---

*The complications parentheses allow, at least in the work of Geoffrey Hill, have been exhaustively explored by Christopher Ricks in "The Tongue's Atrocities," reprinted in his *The Force of Poetry* (Oxford, 1984).

of meter and rhyme, allow her a moral weight the shallow sub-
jects could not supply.

> Light falls from the left. Or so
> it falls in the chambers of Vermeer,
> as even now in this office, where
>
> a six-by-nine glossy print is tacked
> above a desk, high in a city
> that has no place on the valanced map
>
> on the wall of the painted girl. The quaint
> sprawl of that projected shape
> is another world she's never seen—
>
> no, apparently she's seen not much
> of anything, the laughing girl
> who sits an arm's length away,
>
> a window's width of sun, from the faceless
> officer. Who can deny,
> studying them, the historical rift
>
> in every experience of the sexes?
>
> (" 'Officer and Laughing Girl' ")

Like Bishop, Salter urges the argument forward, not just in the
studied ambiguity of "painted girl" or "faceless officer," but in
more modest and ultimately more traitorous adjectives, like
"quaint" sprawl or, elsewhere in the poem, his "jaunty" hat. The
reversals of feeling—this laughter is not something to laugh
about—are not without support from the reversals of rhetoric:
"Light falls from the left. Or so / it falls in the chambers," "no,
apparently she's seen not much / of anything." A neutral ob-
server is finally a faceless one; and Salter's poetry, like Bishop's,
is a poetry of personality, however much it concentrates outside
the self.

Salter's most attractive work, even her most original work
(the most original poetry often builds most obviously on a
predecessor), has inherited its bravura from Bishop. There are
other echoes—Richard Wilbur, Marianne Moore, and Gjer-
trud Schnackenberg (influence between contemporaries is no-
toriously illegible, but the schoolgirlish religious awe of "For
an Italian Cousin" shares a clear identity with Schnackenberg's

tangled Christianity). Salter does not yet possess the artistic re-
sources of these poets. Her "Bee's Elegy" and the mock-grave
poem for her cat ("For I will consider my kitten, Herb"—not
just mock-grave but mock-Smart) descend despite their light-
heartedness into mere posturing, while her elegy for John Len-
non, despite its atrocious puns ("The studio / of history can
tamper with you now, / as if there'd always been a single track /
/ chance traveled on"), is all too serious and thus all too ludi-
crous: "It put you in the headlines once again: / years after
you'd left the band, you joined / another—of those whose lives,
in breaking, link // all memory with their end." The play on
band conjures up JFK on lead guitar and Martin Luther King on
drums. When her poems are written more privately, their self-
satisfaction turns saccharine, their complacence coy—her love
poems are insufferably self-regarding.

The Japanese poems that close this book explore an alien
culture in terms that make the explorer alien and the culture
matter-of-fact. Their exoticism is appealing, however close to
patronizing caricature they tread; but there is too much to recog-
nize, too much to see, and the poems cannot intensify the mass
of visual experience. Even the mental experience has its mono-
tones, unusually for this most controlled of poets—an apprecia-
tion of learning Japanese threatens to go on longer than the
process itself. Beneath the disturbing variety of the present
there exists, as so often for Salter, the security of the past, how-
ever travestied by fashion:

Welcome to Hiroshima

is what you first see, stepping off the train:
a billboard brought to you in living English
by Toshiba Electric. While a channel
silent in the TV of the brain

projects those flickering re-runs of a cloud
that brims its risen columnful like beer
and, spilling over, hangs its foamy head,
you feel a thirst for history: what year

it started to be safe to breathe the air,
and when to drink the blood and scum afloat
on the Ohta River. But no, the water's clear,
they pour it for your morning cup of tea.

This passionate and moral anger, in the other poems not absent so much as unaroused, sweeps away the wry smugness so many of these poems are built on:

> in the case
> adjacent, an exhibit under glass
>
> is glass itself: a shard the bomb slammed in
> a woman's arm at eight-fifteen, but some
> three decades on—as if to make it plain
> hope's only as renewable as pain,
>
> and as if all the unsung
> debasements of the past may one day come
> rising to the surface once again—
> worked its filthy way out like a tongue.

The final image, however disgusting or unpleasant, warns that much that has been silent in this poet may now begin to speak.

Chronicle of the Mideighties

Louise Glück

Even for an American poet, Louise Glück is violently self-centered. The narrow, intense poems of *The Triumph of Achilles* question the fictions of the self until those fictions collapse. Her lines are plain and almost unadorned, as if even the mildest metaphor were dangerous ornament: "Today, when I woke up, I asked myself / why did Christ die? Who knows / the meaning of such questions?" The life too oppressively experienced to be rendered in more than psychological shorthand is reduced to parables, translations from a language harsh and deracinated.

> She taught him the gods. Was it teaching? He went on
> hating them, but in the long evenings of obsessive talk,
> as he listened, they became real. Not that they changed.
> They never came to seem innately human.
> In the firelight, he watched her face.
> But she would not be touched; she had rejected
> the original need. Then in the darkness he would lead her
>   back—
> above the trees, the city rose in a kind of splendor
> as all that is wild comes to the surface.

The prose turns every poem into the purgatory of an argument, all curves of meaning become the straight lines of declamation. In her first book, *Firstborn* (1968), there was a shocking innocence to this doom-ridden, myth-eaten poetry, a luminous outer life stripped away to the sins within. With each succeeding book her voice has darkened—her insights now have the caginess of calculation. Their lack of ease means to prove their sincerity, but their need to prove makes proof impossible.

Only a few poets, like Sylvia Plath, have converted fixation into a poetry that makes the reader feel culpable. Glück now welcomes the brutality love requires: "I felt / hot wax on my forehead. / I wanted it to leave a mark: / that's how I knew I loved you. / Because I wanted to be burned, stamped." She uses her masochism to punish her desires, since what is desired may be despised ("I hate sex, / the man's mouth / sealing my mouth, . . . / the low, humiliating / premise of union"). Her poetry revels in making its mortifications public, and a religious mania has begun to suffuse a poetry whose presiding god was once the god of the uncanny. The ironies allowed are ambivalent: "Our full hearts—at the time, they seemed so impressive. / / Cries, moans, our important suffering." The extremes of such poetry appall even while they compel.

Brad Leithauser

Brad Leithauser's early poems, collected in *Hundreds of Fireflies* (1982), signaled the commitment to traditional form that has lately begun to alter some of the expectations, and some of the illusions, of his contemporaries. *Cats of the Temple* continues Leithauser's enthusiastic regard for animals, and no American since Marianne Moore has shown such insouciant imagination while engaging the nonhuman. Even stuffed like the tortoise ("that tough, undersized head // yearned to outstrip its ponderous cargo") or caged like the ostrich ("the enlarged, enraged glare / of the born disciplinarian"), his animals offer exemplary lessons in persistence and restraint.

Leithauser is a moral poet, as well as a moralist, and his work repeatedly names the conflict between city and country, nurture and nature. His poems depend on their privileged observers, detachment specified in their distance: they watch "the dim / Billowing arms of kelp" from a pier, the city of Kobe from a plane, the deep coral gardens off Guam from the surface forty feet above. In their withdrawal from action, their quiet argument for the contemplative life, his poems register an Augustinian refusal to be drawn to the culture they were formed by. That rejection is made in full knowledge of the city's attractions. There is regret even for its transient glamour, the beauty of the "mad neon dazzle of the Ginza" reflected in an old moat:

> Yet as the duck, in passing,
>
> transforms into a swan, the shapely *S*
> of the neck lit in sudden fluorescent profile,
> and familiar designs begin to coalesce
> within the moat, which soon again will reflect

composedly, you'll grant that while the static
glaze was restful, welcome is this
queen of birds with the sea-serpentine neck,
who trails behind her such thrilling rubble.

Leithauser's designs don't always deepen toward such uneasy epiphanies. These poems are too fond of their surface dazzle, their whimsy and indulgent wordplay ("the instant's / instance," "this mailed male," "settling / *in in an inn*"). The worst poems are exercises in minor wit that might have been left in the exercise book. For a poet who wants the effect as much as the aftereffect, too many of his lines are commonplace or casual. Though this is a book of less formal pressure and less imaginative ambition than his first, Leithauser inhabits a world that has broken with the petty particularities of the self. He brings, especially to the poems set in Japan, a rare delicacy and self-effacement. That is no mild achievement in a self-ridden time.

Richard Kenney

The thematic richness and technical demands of Richard Kenney's first book, *The Evolution of the Flightless Bird* (1984), introduced the baroque course of an unusual imagination. Straitened by his meter and the rashness of his rhyme, he took his satisfactions from science and history, subjects poetry is usually content to ignore. *Orrery* is even more ambitious, the entire book one complex and precocious instrument linking the lives on a cider-milling farm in Vermont to the stars and seasons through the small planetary apparatus, the orrery, that can wheel forward and backward in time, always keeping the planets in their just alignments. The conceit gears each life to another life, each poem to another poem, confining to Newton's orderly and outmoded universe the circuits of human design.

The book's first section, a series of sonnets jammed and bewildered with information, is fraught with the involutions of physics and memory: "The atom's eve? A simple clockwork / world, this farm, where evening stars and drifting quarks / spin lazily across the dark according / to the Laws—if Laws aren't blown to tesserae, / all microchips, a chance, a loss." These are followed by a long sequence tracking the trajectories of farm life through the six seasons of one New England year—the four familiar ones and two extra called Locking and Unlocking, or Hunting and Sugar. The seasons remain in their fixed order, but individual scenes may shift from year to year, granting the annual rituals of labor an Emersonian transcendence to match their pastoral sentiment:

> how small night-blooming orchids
> touch the sticky gobbet of their pollen
> to the feeding hawk moth's compound eye,
> as how this night has touched its opalescent
> moon against the many convex facets
> of the window bay, each whorl and lens
> reflecting back, and how the night sky
> spilling through this house with dusty wings,
> with wind, will find us in another Lenten
> season, you and I, another fast
> broken, another winter come to spring.

The book closes with riddling poems in a two-stress measure not much attempted, and not much mastered, since Auden. Kenney's verbal flourishes are usually harnessed to the work at hand, his extravagance more the fault of ebullience than affectation. In his first book a poet does, in his second he overdoes; and here the grand, unwieldy conceit threatens to overwhelm its frail rural subject. Without the supporting universe of action and interaction, the individual poems read more like diary than design. The poet genially neglects the harsh or sordid aspects of farm life; his characters, simple-hearted but not simpleminded, are unequal to the technician's vocabulary (*glair, calvarium, circination, strake, shako, seiche, coign, chyme,* and, more amusingly, the misspelled *concensus* and *morraine*). Kenney is measured by ambition: the ruin of this book displays, radiantly, the gifts of intelligence and language that are his to control.

Linda Gregg

The cool progress of Linda Gregg's sentences is fractured by emotion beneath the surface: "I stood watching the great hulk of desire / glide within memory. Watched it move / like the only true beauty in the world. Let it pass." The simple perceptions lead-weighted with abstraction, the almost involuntary stutter, the sentences purged of subjects: this is a rhetoric fully calculated in dissociation and discontent. In *Alma* her stories are half-stories, half-lit scenes, half-remembered gestures, where nothing can be said, nothing survived.

> I see no way to survive the soul's journey.
> At the beginning, we are like angels
> painted around the Madonna. Conceived
> in safety, in the freshness of our bodies.
> As we age, wisdom can be heard climbing
> the stairs blindly under the bare bulb
> groping for a string which we know how
> to find in the dark only if we have
> practiced delicately meanwhile.

Gregg is too easily attracted to such beautiful but windy fabulism, too easily lured into doggerel: "Far is where I am near. / Far is where I live. / My house is in the far. / The night is still. / A dog barks from a farm." The attempt to charge every gesture with meaning makes all her gestures suspect. The sentences so fresh and freshly troubled in her first book, *Too Bright to See* (1981), have softened into emotional excess, an excess no more evident than in an elegy that fails for two dozen lines to reveal the object of grief is a rabbit.

However unbridled in emotional demand, Gregg aspires to a poetry ascetic in its attenuation. Her better work doesn't resist the incomplete, but uses it to subvert her terrors—in a poem about a copperhead, "Almost blind he takes the soft dying / into the muscle-hole of his haunting. / The huge jaws eyeing, the raised head sliding / back and forth, judging the exact place of his killing." Though here it slips into quiet parody of Longfellow or Robinson, her work's eccentric aggression cannot allow rhetoric to become rhetorical posture. The heartlessness that distinguishes this poetry also haunts it, and there is little evidence the conditions that create the poet's turmoil will allow her any restraint.

Howard Moss

Howard Moss's reputation has been the shadow of accomplishment. As poetry editor of the *New Yorker,* he has for more than thirty years occupied a position of literary authority, though that position must often have seemed a devil's bargain. Ignored by critics who feared to offend, his poetry has paid the price of prominence, though his critics have not been wholly at fault. Thick with the influence of Auden, Moss's first poems did not survive the compromise of their conventions. His slight, almost decorative talent turned toward stanzas placidly contrived without an original thought—or, rather, where the original thoughts had all been clothed in period manner. A poet's early work teaches his readers how to misread his later; and a pervasive blandness infected Moss's early poems like the flu.

Moss gradually overthrew these limited burdens and unlimited ingratiations, setting his subjects in a life alternating between urbane whim and urban dread. His violence was a life of appointments, at the masseur's or in the x-ray room. He could write, "We worked for years / Only to arrive at deeper mysteries," because his longer poems became the record of a life lived, no longer a life imagined. What survived as his poetry matured were the passions acknowledged but constrained—even the poems of disappointed love sounded only their note of disappointment, of regret and not ruin.

A poet must at least occasionally pretend to ruin. In his two most recent books, the most fully represented in these *New Selected Poems,* Moss's poetry has taken full advantage of his detachment, recording the merely ornamental with the harsh world in which ornament survives:

> Last night the moon had a Byzantine flare
> Of lemon gold like the goldleaf halos
> One sees in the early Italian masters—
> Venice, in fact, comes to mind, the palazzos'
> Sandcastle, ice-cream feats, effects
> Childish but pleasing, of spun-stone heights,
> While a rat stands gnawing a lettuce leaf
> At the edge of one of the canals.

The fears of this world are the more unsettling in the calmness of their recognition. His poetry hovers at the edge of disaster, where the pastoral has been ravaged ("the lopsided barn, / Abandoned hayrick, and broken silo / Make clear once again

that Paradise / Is a place that must be left behind") and the city
spoiled past redemption or repair, as in this vision of Miami
Beach:

> A watering hole abandoned by the young,
> Either the old will take it over
> Completely or South American money
>
> Found its new capital: a *kitsch* Brasilia
> Of pre-stressed concrete with its air-conditioned
> Swiss bank branch, and a single restored
>
> Art deco hotel for absentee landlords
> Scanning the sea rehearsing endlessly
> Its threatened drama never to be performed.

In Moss's work art is always immanent in nature. It is the civiliz-
ing mark of his later poetry that even faced with the apocalypse
he would see only a moment of terrible beauty.

On Forms of Feeling

John Hollander

Two poets coexist in John Hollander, one a master of the modulations of form, sensitive to the sensual effect of language and the sexual demand of image. That poet contributes the most lambently feeling poems to *Harp Lake*—the harp lake is the Sea of Galilee, and a number of poems here derive from a visit to Jerusalem. The elegant quatrains of "Kinneret" (from Yam Kinneret, the sea's Hebrew name) move from the regret of shattered love and a life "whose every task is botched" through the reconciliations of landscape—a landscape that blood has repeatedly purchased—toward the humility of self-recognition.

> Pale cliffs descend below the sea and steep
>   In the full silence, calm and unconfounded.
> He broke through the thrumming surface of his sleep
>   As if some lake-shaped instrument had sounded.

The other poet is a critic's darling, not a master but a monster of form who cannot forgo any opportunity to flaunt his erudition or self-consciousness, who will ruin any mood to prove how artificial a poetic mood is. Stiff, dry, intellective, mannered, he is allowed to interrupt even the sensual progress of "Kinneret" ("I stop—something is too pedestrian / About the iambs in this kind of meter") in a senseless rhetorical gaffe. Hollander is an intemperately gifted scholar whose *Vision and Resonance* (1975) and *The Figure of Echo* (1981) are permanent contributions to discussion of the art, but whose poetry has been cursed by the knowing gifts of his scholarship.

Too often Hollander's work descends to intellectual exercise. At home in any style, he is out of place in them all. *Harp Lake* is full of poems on paintings or drawings, poems on whimsical occasions, poems on the art of art, and even one of his well-known "shaped" poems, the poetical equivalent of topiary. Most of these are highly polished and not much given to the lubrications of feeling. In "To the Rokeby Venus," however, one of his teasing exercises in double entendre (his *Town and Country Mat-*

ters [1972] may be the only interesting book of erotic poetry this century), in the lovely canzone "Island Pond," in the informal hexameter of "By the Gulf" and the friendly formalities of "Ballade for Richard Wilbur," Hollander challenges the forms of the formal poets of his generation. It takes a strong character to raise the artificial to the heights of art.

Rachel Hadas

In 1972 Rachel Hadas operated an olive-oil press on the island of Samos. One night there was a fire, and two years later Hadas and a codefendant were acquitted of arson. Biography here is relevant to art; without it the poem about her trial might seem completely allegorical. Biography forces these poems toward a factual center, just as the occasion of rhyme and meter forces them toward a formal one. For those still able to savor the pleasures of rhyme, she offers a number of poems that in elegant self-gratification are reminiscent of James Merrill.

> Say that you're lying comfortably under
> the weather. Outside world? A passer-by
> whose shadow barely skims the lukewarm puddle
> of reverie you drown in as you lie.
>
> Bruised but not feverish, you stretch and drowse,
> minimally drugged against the pain.
> An opalescent country's taking shape:
> carpet, oasis, palms, a golden plain.

It is rare these days, at least among poets under fifty, to find a poet whose syntax is not inferior to her intelligence. Unfortunately the forms are not embraced with any consistency, and Hadas is as likely to write with formal elegance as without any elegance at all. A boy can be made to say, during the 1974 coup d'état, "We shit on all the beaches. / Remoteness of tender flesh. / I am at a distance from my life." The author can begin a pantoum:

> The goldenrod sheds pollen in the butter.
> The lawnmower, just before it stops, goes sputter.
> The valleys echo roars from the wood cutter.
> I write a word down; mouth it; finally utter.

She can say about feeding cattle, "I kiss your velvet muzzle, / I bathe in your warm urine, oh my sister," or disclose, in an excess of intimacy, "That was the year of my persistent hemorrhoid." Even words or syllables can break up: "syl by a by ble / silly bull sibyl able sibling label." Context cannot salvage these embarrassments.

These poems arrest a careering from country to country, from instability to instability. Hadas writes most vulnerably of a Greek landscape noticed only obliquely, when cleaning fish ("The waves look small. They suck away and under / whatever stolen iridescences / I scrape off with my rusty knife") or turning away from someone ("I vaguely see / the flat port town from the bungalow window. Brave / new world gone dry and flyblown in September / that gleamed in June"). The careering never frees the author from herself. In a poem about her trial, the prosecutor's monologue is witty and terrifying, while hers is theatrical and unconvincing. She convicts herself—at least of writing ill a defense that's gone for good.

Rhyme is the leap of perception that frees Hadas from biography. Form is never all things to all, but to such a poet it is the final condition of the imaginative act. Her poems after her return to the States favor a homely domesticity too cozy for drama, and she begins to let the form speak to the form, producing poems as tediously self-regarding as poems about poetry usually are. Only surrounded by the alien can she be most at home.

The Old Campaigner

William Meredith comes to his second book of selected poems as member of the American Academy and Institute of Arts and Letters, former chancellor of the Academy of American Poets, former Consultant in Poetry to the Library of Congress. Such a career, for a minor poet (as Meredith modestly describes himself), has already begun to sink under the accumulated weight of position and honor. *Partial Accounts* is an adeptly deprecative and diffident title, especially if the accounts are secret, numbered, and Swiss, not merely narrative. Like many poets, Meredith has been most ruthless toward his earliest work, and the already narrow selection he made from his first two volumes for *Earth Walk: New and Selected Poems* (1970) has thinned a little further. Indeed, his "Homeric Simile," once a sign of epic ambition, has lost its Homeric designation and its last lines as well.

No one blames a poet for concealing early flaws, since later ones often suffer by comparison. The myth of artistic progress—last work, best work—lets no poet favor his first books over his last. The necessary myth allows the writer to go on writing, but it is not harmless. It authorizes the only violence, after revision, a poet is conscionably permitted. Archibald MacLeish, in his introduction to Meredith's first volume, *Love Letter from an Impossible Land* (1944, chosen as MacLeish's first selection for the Yale Series of Younger Poets), already recognized Meredith's "quality of reticence" and "almost unwilling communication." Erasure is the only fulfillment of reticence.

Meredith's first book, written under condition of war, was an exercise, and often an exercise in early Auden.

> Laughing young man and fiercest against sham,
>   Then you have stayed at sea, at feckless sea,
>   With a single angry curiosity
> Savoring fear and faith and speckled foam?
>   ("In Memoriam Stratton Christensen")

> Limped out of the hot sky a hurt plane,
> Held off, held off, whirring pretty pigeon,

> Hit then and scuttled to a crooked stop.
> The stranger pilot who emerged
>
> ("Navy Field")

was Wystan Auden, fresh from *The Orators,* clutch of syntax, archaic inversion, and feckless adjectives intact. Meredith had the advantage of actually being a Navy pilot; but the actual is not always convincing when style imposes upon it, and Auden's style was superbly adapted to the symbolic gesture, not the ground crew. The heroic pathos of the air war was more harshly realized by Randall Jarrell, who washed out as a pilot and never saw combat. At his worst, Meredith reduces the war to a series of elegant miniatures, where an aircraft carrier "troubles the waters, and they part and close / Like a people tired of an old queen / Who has made too many progresses," where "the bomb's luck, the gun's poise and chattering, / The far-off dying, are her near affair." They might concern a love affair for all their engagement with the carnage and clotted blood.

Those passages come from *Ships and Other Figures* (1948), which was followed by a ten-year hiatus. *The Open Sea and Other Poems* (1958) claimed not least in its first adjective that the wars, including the wars with his predecessors, were over. When poets come into the open, however, they often inherit flaws with their favors, making treaty with their influences on unfavorable terms. If *The Open Sea* was the first book of Meredith's maturity, it was also where his special defects and limitations, as opposed to the defects and limitations of his models, became apparent:

> With flanks as clean as bone they signal one another
> On the far side of a trench of music—
> Such breasts and hair, such bold genitals.
>
> ("The Ballet")

The failures lie deep in the phrase, in those signaling flanks. The tone, at once prissy and pretentious, has gone drastically wrong even before the gaze moves downward to those comic genitals (and perhaps in *trench* the war has not been left completely behind). Meredith's early work, and much of his later, abounds in such casual clumsiness, where intelligence attempts to bear the imaginative act. A poet so self-conscious—he always seems to be watching his feet—is given to fetal poems about poems ("It is this way with verse and animals / And love, that when you point you lose them all"), not the invention of our century but surely its weakness. Elsewhere the lines grind with effort and effect ("His thoughts concenter there monotonously," "Soughing together in divine remorse"); the period diction that poets like Lowell narrowly skirted slows into the turgidity that menaced it.

Those were the flaws; the favors were more unexpected. Like Spender (in relation to his junior, Auden), Meredith accepted at the start of his maturity his subsidiary position; he abandoned to his seniors (Lowell, Berryman, Jarrell) their fatal ambitions. Freed of the rhetoric of grand statement, his poems developed an ease of expression both quiet and compelling. One senses the effort by which ease was attained, and occasionally what was compelled was something hideously close to the regional verse of newspapers ("There is no end to the / Deception of quiet things / And of quiet, everyday / People a lifetime brings"). Such newspapers, however, would never permit verse of this lightness and authority:

> A person is very self-conscious about his head.
> It makes one nervous just to know it is cast
> In enduring materials, and that when the real one is dead
> The cast one, if nobody drops it or melts it down, will last.
>
> We pay more attention to the front end, where the face is,
> Than to the interesting and involute interior:
> The Fissure of Rolando and such queer places
> Are parks for the passions and fears and mild hysteria.
>
> The things that go on there! Erotic movies are shown
> To anyone not accompanied by an adult.
> The marquee out front maintains a superior tone:
> Documentaries on Sharks and The Japanese Tea Cult.
> ("Thoughts on One's Head")

The poem continues for four stanzas not nearly as distinguished, but Meredith's earlier work lacked such humor: its wordplay was wormy with its own gravity. When Meredith abandoned the tragic stage in its tragic rhetoric, he discovered the virtues beneath vanity; and his verse became consequent to the forces that had victimized it. He was able to convert his clumsy self-consciousness to comic effect or conceal it in persona. The former strategy produced "Thoughts on One's Head," the latter a luminous translation from Corbière ("Letter from Mexico"). They were the first poems that seemed a crucial matter to the poet, that did not carry out a distasteful duty with cold solemnity.

That change in poetic address uncovered the deeper anxieties in *The Wreck of the Thresher and Other Poems* (1964) and the new poems included in *Earth Walk*. Read against later successes of understatement, the subject of the early poems is their own inflated grandeur. Even afterward, whenever the Public Man threatens, the style thickens like a sauce. Here the dead men of the Thresher speak: "Study something deeper than yourselves, / As, how the heart, when it turns diver, delves and saves." Here the Capitol is described: "The dome at the top of the hill, heavy with reference, / is iron out of the soil, yearned up as if it were white stone, / the way for a time our thought and rhetoric yearned upward." Yearned upward, indeed.

Contrast with these marble fragments of epigraphy the delicate etching, at once acid and affectionate, of Mrs. Leamington in "Roots," the longest poem of Meredith's middle period. The speaker's visit at first seems cast as one of Eliot's arch pieces of vers de société ("Mrs. Leamington stood on a cloud, / Quarreling with a dragon—it was May, / When things tend to look allegorical"). When Mrs. Leamington rather battily asks, "Have you ever really thought about the roots. . . ?," the speaker is so cunningly responsive that any pretension in her world might easily be punctured:

> I'd thought about them
> All the week before, when the elms were budding,
> The twigs so delicate we might have had
> A Chinese landscapist for first selectman
> Who put out all the town roads to wild plum.
> In a week they would be plain leafy elms—
> Not a gross thing to be, god knows, but coarser.

Just at the point where one's sympathy for this encounter would thin (the rich *are* different, after all—they're more boring), Mrs. Leamington drifts into thoughts of mortality:

"I've been thinking about dying," she went on.
"I'll be seventy-four this summer, so I ought to.
Some of my mother's people are right here,
On this place, I mean, just across the road.
It used to be a graveyard. There are beech trees
All around it and a view up-river.
Maybe I'll have them put me there intact;
I used to say I'd like to drift as ashes
Over the fields, and give them that much back.
But more and more I think of the beech roots
Holding up stones like blossoms or like nests
Or like the colored stones on a jade tree—
That slope was never cleared, it's mostly stones—
And in the lower branches, a tree-house:
A box in the ground where I meet my own image sleeping,
The soft brown branches raising it aloft—
Except aloft is down or I sleep face down.
Well, back to my spuds, she said. Don't you hate that word?
Yet it's good Middle English. Stop on your way home.
By then perhaps we'll both have earned a drink."

This passage secures its pathos, and the lovely downward inverted image of the roots, while leaving the prickly character intact. It is difficult to prevent such a poem, so much at the mercy of its character's attitudes and its author's prejudices, as well as the great mastering example of Frost, from falling into contrivance or condescension. To such effect Meredith's suppression of self is an advantage.

In other poems that advantage is less evident—the author stands aside, as he stood aside for Mrs. Leamington, but the stage remains empty and dark. Meredith's life has been so well shielded, banished to an Augustan shade, that his reticence is the veneer of poems that speak indirectly of a life and its limits. In this as in other ways he is reminiscent of Jarrell—not saving his seriousness with wit, but earning it through Yeatsian earnestness. Both men were born with barely an ounce of natural poetic talent, the sort that makes even a minor line of Lowell's memorable. One expects more of a man and his mind than Meredith is willing to give—the aggressive denial of character allows him to be possessed by other poets. Meredith told Frost of night landings on a carrier during the war. Frost's response was as convenient as it was cutting: "I'd respect you / For that if for nothing else." How did Meredith repay the veiled insult? By allowing Frost to swallow him whole:

> My loud machine for making hay
> Mutters about our work today.
> Through bushes and small trees it flails—
> Blueberry, sumac, cherry, bay.
>
> I lay the little woods in swales
> To burn them as the daylight fails
> For no surviving horse or cow
> Is fed such crazy salad bales.
>
> They fall like jackstraws, anyhow,
> Or like the forest, trunk and bough
> That harder hands and will than these
> Burned once, where it is meadow now.
>
> I side with meadow against trees
> Because of woodsmoke in the breeze,
> The ghost of other foes—though both
> Would find us puny enemies,
> Second growth and second growth.
> ("An Old Field Mowed for Appearances' Sake")

Such confident ventriloquism is different from wrestling with an influence—it is the influence itself, the movement completely unmediated: homespun, diligent, and wholly unoriginal (but wittily honest about its status as "second growth"). Submission is the most beautiful and dangerous form of homage. In *Hazard, the Painter* (1975), Meredith succumbed entirely to temptation. Meredith's Hazard is Berryman's Henry, after a sea change to the suburbs. Meredith's deep reserve may crave an alter ego, even someone else's alter ego, but the transparent guise of his renaming flawed Hazard at the start, creature of chance or mischance, contrived obstacle or literary accident.

> I look out of these two holes, or I run
> into the other two and listen. Is Hazard trapped in here?
>
> I have had on this funny suit for years, it's getting
> baggy, but I can still move all the parts.

In the top I can make satisfying noises.
I fill it again & again with things I want.
It does not like them all. I empty it furtively.

It is rubbery and durable, I wash it.
People sometimes touch it, that feels good
although I am deep inside.

                    ("Where He's Staying Now")

Henry's sometimes unbearable baby talk has been echoed with pointless fidelity. Though Meredith means Hazard both to be and to excoriate the au courant, indulging periodically in political rant (much of it now pruned), the painter is a mild mannerist, not a raging abstract expressionist. The flimsiest persona may bring forth the most tormented confession, if there is tormented confession to be made; but Meredith is finally too reasonable, too aware of his own absurdity, to take advantage of his creation or do justice to it. The mask labors forth a middle-class professional, full of genial mortalities. The psychology of this literary act, full of mock penance and mild plagiarism, is acute.

Meredith's recent poetry, in *The Cheer* (1980) and the new poems collected here, is a short study in imaginative fatigue. The poet's interest has not shrunk completely to his own profession, though there are poems about poetry, poems dedicated to poets, poems in honor of dead poets (one for Lowell and three for Berryman), a poem talking back to another poet (W. H. Auden), a poem for Shelley in the voice of Trelawny, and a poem with a poetic epigraph (*two dozen* lines from Robert Penn Warren) longer than the poem itself. There is even a poem, titled "Poem," about a poem of Yeats's. What might have been an extended consideration of the craft rises merely into the philosophy of chat:

> Against evil, between evils, lovely words are right.
> How absurd it would be to spin these noises out,
> so serious that we call them poems,
> if they couldn't make a person smile.
> Cheer or courage is what they were all born in.
> It's what they're trying to tell us, miming like that.

                    ("The Cheer")

In these late poems Meredith strains toward an intimacy so inept it can only seem insincere. The "minor poet / for sixty-three years in America" now contents himself with dropping names: "There's no heat in the house of course in May / unless I light a fire. Stevens / I think would have lighted one today / and, comfortable with my betters, I do too." Few fictional characters manage quite so easy a transition between complacency and unctuousness. How strange, then, that amid poems that contrive to be maudlin about American government there are passages with a composure rarely before apparent:

> The farm dogs bark at a soft crash far up-river:
> the ice-breaker is coming down. We go out
> in the clear night to see the lights—beacons
> on the river, pharos in the sky, and a jewelled
> seafarer bringing water to the parched plain.
> The hollow roar grows slower than an avalanche.
> Her search-light feeling a way from point
> of land to point of land, she pulls herself along
> by beacon-roots. For a half-mile reach of river
> she sights on us, a group of goblins blinking
> in front of their white house. Sugary rime
> feathers from the bow. An emerald and a garnet
> flank the twitching eye.
>
> ("Winter on the River")

The sugary ease of phrasing, the almost effortless drive of image toward feeling not forced or advertised, hint at qualities this poet has mistaken or misused. Like Howard Moss and other "minor poets" of this generation, Meredith has perfected certain tones unavailable to poets of more severe ambition or temperament. There may yet be more attention paid, when even the suburbs have come to seem quaint, to poets who attempted to make terms with the mild malaise of American life. To have slaved so long in the second rank of American poetry and be rewarded with not one poem fit for the anthologies of the next century might seem mean repayment. One can offer nothing less than respect for such real if not distinctive achievements, and one can offer nothing more. The last stanza of *Partial Accounts* betrays an attitude lethal to serious poetic ambition: "For the moment, though, you are holding this poem. / Its aim is that of any artifact: to ingratiate."

Old Masters

Seamus Heaney

The title sequence of *Station Island,* Seamus Heaney's new book, is a series of "dream encounters with familiar ghosts," figures therefore twice ghostly. A young priest off to his death in the tropics, a Latin schoolmaster, a friend murdered in a robbery—these allow Heaney the stories of an Irish past, excuses for narrative in a book that everywhere struggles for lyric. The tension between lyric nature and narrative necessity informs the struggle between Heaney and his language, as it may inform the vexed nature of Irish life. What the past rescues for the present are not lives exceptional, only allegorical, yoking the fallen nature of the present to a fallen past, a state of absolute sin to a state of sin mitigated or governed, but no less violent:

> I who learned to read in the reek of flax
> and smelled hanged bodies rotting on their gibbets
> and saw their looped slime gleaming from the sacks—
>
> hard-mouthed Ribbonmen and Orange bigots
> made me into the old fork-tongued turncoat
> who mucked the byre of their politics.

As Odysseus knew, one learns from the dead the position of the living.

The ghosts invoked elsewhere include mad Sweeney, the king whose legend Heaney translated in *Sweeney Astray* (1984). Taking on the mantle of the king allows the past to rise into the poet: in this mixture of modern and medieval there is something of the intelligent regard for both worlds that characterized Geoffrey Hill's *Mercian Hymns* (1971).

> I was a lookout posted and forgotten.
>
> On one side under me, the concrete road.
> On the other, the bullocks' covert,
> the breath and plaster of a drinking place
> where the school-leaver discovered peace
> to touch himself in the reek of churned-up mud.

Poems continually infuse these poems, as language itself does ("the brush of a word like *peignoir*, // rustles and glimpses, shot silk," "Haunting the granaries of words like *breasts*"). Heaney believes everything resolves through language, a virtuous if romantic position in a culture riven by a religious violence also linguistic and political, that turns on the nature of home: "the words of coming to rest: // *birthplace, roofbeam, whitewash, / flagstone, hearth,* / like unstacked iron weights." Like Ovid and Dante, other poets driven from their cities by politics, Heaney makes home a moral argument, a place whose attractions are resisted even as they are acknowledged and embraced.

Heaney's poems about language heave toward their linguistic resolutions, as if poetry were not sufficient answer to his quarrels with the tongue—poems about poetry suffer Zeno's paradox, prevented by constant self-examination from arriving at poetry itself. Heaney has always been a poet for whom eating and devouring are central metaphors, his language taking on a voluptuary pleasure whenever food is mentioned: seizing a lobster, "we plunged and reddened it." The language itself is plunged and reddened—Heaney is the most sensual poet of language since Lowell, whose tones he sometimes honors by imitation.

That pleasure in the working sound of words explains the impulse toward making a precision through an imprecision, giving two adjectives because one will not serve: "polished sloes, bitter / and dependable," "the hampered one, out of water, / fortified and bewildered," "A hit-man on the brink, emptied and deadly." The rigor of such attention is carried into the moral frame of literature. That is not to argue that all art ought to be moral any more than all morality should derive from art; but in Heaney's poetry the place of morality in civilized discourse is not forgotten or ignored, as has been too convenient for too long in the practice of his contemporaries. He refuses to write for this time alone.

Gjertrud Schnackenberg

Gjertrud Schnackenberg is the most technically astute and most technically privileged poet of her generation, the generation now in its thirties. The American poetry that for the past fifteen or twenty years has found its subjects at home, no more daring than a diary, and its style in a prose of exquisite sameness, has been challenged by the formal verse of Schnackenberg and others. It is not a revolution so much as the radicalism of a return. Like all new fashions, it attracts poets whose intelligence could not be exhausted, or even sufficiently tested, by the current etiquette of poetic composition. It has made much current practice seem immediately outmoded and dull.

Schnackenberg is a poet exercised by lives, particularly artistic lives, if artistic can mean a life that discovers its own conclusions. Chopin in exile, Darwin the year before his death, the painter Ivan Generalić after the death of his wife, Simone Weil starving, even Sleeping Beauty before she wakes—these are lives that have arrived at the cusp of disaster or renewal, that in their endings deepen the tyranny of time:

> In the city of slaves to mirrors, of rivalries
> Championed for less than a day by charlatans,
> Of politics lending heat to the rented rooms
> Of exiled virtuosos, and of cholera warnings affixed
> To the posts of the streetlamps, whose heads
> Flare with fever from here to the outermost districts.

The scene is Chopin's, but even the ageless dreaming of Sleeping Beauty does not lessen the hour's possessiveness, at least for a kitchen maid whose lover is stranded outside the castle frozen in time.

The fourteen poems of *The Lamplit Answer* complicate the attractions of Schnackenberg's first book, *Portraits and Elegies* (1982), taking from a variety of forms the resources each contains. She moves through them with equal assurance and equal occasion. Where Auden found each form a new excuse for the peculiar wit of his intelligence, Schnackenberg compels the form to test the limits of sensibility. The fictionalized biography of Chopin requires a rich free verse, an incident in Darwin's life the irregular lines of rhymed quatrains, a poem on "Supernatural Love" rhymed triplets. Her love poems celebrate an affair so deep the poet must torture them to humor, when such a love can never be humored. Even the least of her work, two wicked light-verse pieces about a pair of adversaries, Clumsy and No-No, whether disciple and devil, miniature Faust and Mephistopheles, risks the virtues of form for what the form might serve.

Her desires are often gripped by their images; drawn to redemption and transumption, Schnackenberg's images are brought to light:

> Bayed in the lap of the Marchioness, the littlest
> And most charming monkey in Paris, who appears
> To have crossed childhood's threshold middle-aged,
> Murders a lily, wringing it by the stem,
> Then flings it aside as the recital begins,
> And the powder shaken from the lily's horn
> Scatters like crumbs of fire across the floor.

She is not someone who believes so much as someone who makes believe. The fallen Christianity that haunts her is a Christianity of language—"Supernatural Love" describes a childhood incident in which she calls carnations "Christ's flowers." Her father can make no sense of it until he turns to the dictionary, a dictionary aptly suffused with light. He finds there the lamplit answer, the etymology that links carnations to flesh and nail, to a Passion a four-year-old would know nothing of. Even language can mislead, however—the child's confusion is indirectly and subtly explained only when the word *incarnation* is slyly introduced. The child's prescience about Christ was only a mishearing, and yet from such mishearings a whole religion blossoms.

Schnackenberg uses experience without being weakened by it. While most younger poets inherit a language unable to stretch even to the limits of their limited lives, her language hungers to become experience. One could praise her with a lavishness only her later poems will earn. The verse is still at times too metronomic, the point of view rigid and, though not conventional (it is like no one else's), almost unvarying. Conversant with the gorgeous possibilities of language, with the difficult emotion language contains, she is now a poet necessary for our imaginings.

Amy Clampitt

American poets take little account of the foreign—most American poetry, like American wheat, is only for domestic consumption. In this as in other ways Amy Clampitt has been a beguiling anomaly. Her third book, *Archaic Figure,* plunders the past, and certain foreign precincts of the present, with the energy and erratic efficiency of Lord Elgin and with less destructive result. In her grand tour and Greek mythology, she takes a contrasting measure of "the plinth of what we quaintly call // Our Time," where Medusa rises in George Eliot's life or the doges of Venice reinterpret the sodbusters' vacant Midwest:

> the Bucintoro
> with the Doge afloat, rowed to the cheering
> of lubricious throngs, the whimpering
> of lutes: a stage set above the windings
> of these onetime sloughs, the hidden
> thoroughfares obscure and treacherous
> as the dim wagon tracks the homesteaders
> would inevitably follow into the disguiseless
> grassland.

Such violent juxtapositions, though they risk the anarchy of mere anachronism, provide an engagement with history, the past surviving into the present, absent from poems that simply attempt to reinflate the Macy's parade of mythological figures: Medusa herself, Perseus, Athena. There and in some of Clampitt's travel reports, too, much has been drawn from the detritus of touring, and her lines have not translated the lessons of Bulfinch or the *Guide Bleu.* One can read too often in her expression the carbons of her American Express.

Clampitt's strongest work never loses sight of her severity, or of the idiosyncratic reactions that make her idiosyncratic style more than merely ingenious. By now that style occasionally lapses into mannerism: the long, sometimes wearying sentences; the sharp enjambments that seem a nervous mania; the phrases lined up like boxcars; the vocabulary whirled through a Waring Blendor ("the treetop-filtered / tangerine of dawn, / the zenith's frescoed-by- / Tiepolo cerulean"). Such complaints border on praise, since these stanzas escape the flat prose that afflicts much contemporary poetry. Syntax and diction are the radical forces behind any change in poetic sensibility.

Clampitt is drawn to the dead and the damned, to artists who lived on the social margins. The poems in *Archaic Figure* converge on women, and the goddesses and mythological figures who are their divine representatives, the taint in an untainted past. By such displacements she compiles a book of subtle recognitions, embracing in the other the adequate explanations, or adequate mysteries, of the self. Even the title may be a bit of wry self-mockery: the dust jacket's marble statue has lost its head.

Self-mockery is one of the great attractions of Clampitt's poetic voice. The skeptic who sees the modern fakes in an ancient market responds to the pathos of squalor on the Hellas International Express, four hours late to Munich. Though many of these new poems seem willed and even willful, in her most memorable—a series on the Wordsworths, a lush invocation of Venice—Clampitt fashions from her magpie details a world rich in the corruptions, and corrections, of a life: "this existence, this / botched, cumbersome, much-mended, / not unsatisfactory thing." After one of the most extraordinary late starts in our literature (her first book, *The Kingfisher*, was not published until she was sixty-three), Amy Clampitt has become one of our poetry's sovereign imaginations.

Richard Wilbur

Among the honorable schoolboys of American poetry, Richard Wilbur has often seemed the most cursed by his talent. Clever as a cat, aseptically witty, gifted in the methods of his masters, he was able even in his earliest work to charm his way into favor or chatter out of difficulty. Though most poets eventually leave their sugared sonnets and their scandals behind, a few—W. H. Auden, for example—remain schoolboys into old age, a sly immaturity coexisting happily with the more mature forms of ague and argument.

To suggest that Wilbur is of that company recognizes his peculiar attractions as well as his particular limitations. *New and Collected Poems,* his first collection of new poems in twelve years, does nothing to alter the shape of a career as honored as it has been honorable. The poet laureateship to which he was appointed last year is a bit of American Anglophilia, barely more serious than naming a state insect or a state reptile. Though earned for books published over thirty years ago, the honor was not misplaced.

Wilbur's first book, *The Beautiful Changes* (1947), was charged with highly intellectual and often brittle juvenalia. He embraced rhyme schemes giddy with the display of language, whose effects often exceeded the interest of their subjects. A new postwar tone infused such self-satisfied irrelevance, but the reader was apt to become impatient with poems about the potato, the *Walgvogel* (dodo), or the *mélongène* (eggplant). Despite some brilliantly managed tours de force, the collection's contrived and preposterous phrases have the musty whiff of the academy about them: "her lettuce head all full / Of bawdry and novenas," "a sailingcraft / On heilignüchterne lakes of memory," "one star's synecdochic smirk."

Such insouciance was followed by the increasingly statesmanlike but still fabulously baroque poems of *Ceremony* (1950) and *Things of This World* (1956), where the grand manner was mixed with Grand Marnier:

> The tall camels of the spirit
> Steer for their deserts, passing the last groves loud
> With the sawmill shrill of the locust, to the whole honey of the arid
> Sun. They are slow, proud,
>
> And move with a stilted stride
> To the land of sheer horizon, hunting Traherne's
> *Sensible emptiness,* there where the brain's lantern-slide
> Revels in vast returns.

The sensible pleasure of such images, showy and yet self-consciously deliberate, supplies the convections of a mind that would rather intimate than be intimate. Little of Wilbur's early poetry could be called personal, and none of it troubled, though even the happiest poet may live in a kingdom of discontent. Wilbur often seems the sweet alter ego of Robert Lowell, whose massive formal distortions of language were in the service of subjects more personal and grave. It would be a mistake, however, to believe that a poet of light is one without weight:

> The eyes open to a cry of pulleys,
> And spirited from sleep, the astounded soul
> Hangs for a moment bodiless and simple
> As false dawn.
>   Outside the open window
> The morning air is all awash with angels.

> Some are in bed-sheets, some are in blouses,
> Some are in smocks: but truly there they are.

Few poets could take laundry, and clean laundry at that, as a manifestation of the metaphysical (and then stoop to an insinuating pun in "awash"). Wilbur's most brilliant and ambitious work, like that of mathematicians, was done young. What earlier seemed playful gradually hardened, and the coolly detached tone became complacent and plummy, especially in the shorter poems scattered through his books. He became a poet untrustworthy under sonnet length. The mild disappointments of his later books can be measured only against the grand early architecture. As the intensity of Wilbur's poetry subsided, his attention turned to translation, to which we owe the incomparable renditions of Molière and Racine.

In the autumnal poems newly collected here, sadness and death are the suffusing themes, played against nature and its annual rebirths.

> Shadblow; in farthest air
> Toss three unsettled birds; where naked ledge
> Buckles the surge is a green glare
> Of moss at the water's edge;
>
> And in this eddy here
> A russet disc of maple-pollen spins.
> With such brave poverties the year
> Unstoppably begins.

The courtly movement, without generosity or passion, finds in form the sharpest exaction of emotion. Wilbur was a dangerous influence on the poets of his own generation, few of whom had his gifts; and his influence has continued among the younger poets interested in form, many of whom mimic his light, frivolous air without his skill or daring. With Anthony Hecht and James Merrill, Wilbur maintained a formal tradition when even the *word* "tradition" was suspect. Of the poets of his generation, those born in the decade after World War I, he is among the two or three most vital and surely the most elegant. Randall Jarrell once wrote in a letter, "Not that I don't like Wilbur, but one is enough." No reader will be ungrateful for that one.

Interview

Free verse or form?

My own poems are sheepishly heterodox. Free verse and formal composition have different values, different stringencies, and either may corrupt even the wary talent into vanity. I'm bewildered by the belligerence of their partisans. Some of the masters of the century—Eliot, Pound, Stevens, Lowell, Hill—have been fluent in both but demagogue for neither. Perhaps we are beyond such lessons, but American poetry is not a brave splendid thing that can ignore technique, any technique. Our anthologies are encyclopedias of technique, and they have been written for us by the dead.

But don't you think that for some poets form can be a restriction?

I accept that meter requires submission to an arbitrary power. Poets not practiced in submission feel they cannot speak, that the words will not fall in sympathetic order—the words are tongue-tied. To a poet of metrical form, submission is a liberation—it charts a navigable course through reefs and shoals of jabber. Poets who find their force in form are grateful for the accidents of imagination and the precedents of tradition. Even free-verse poets consider form stripped of meter (in a "postmodern" villanelle or sestina) a shock to the imagination. The free-verse sestina has permanently stolen graces from its metrical counterpart—our ears have become tuned to the violation.

Isn't free verse more intimate? Isn't it closest to everyday speech?

Wouldn't it be pretty to think so? We're haunted by the intimacy of Shakespeare or Donne or Keats. For Wordsworth the "real language of men" was appropriate to the language of meter, at least in the "experiment" of *Lyrical Ballads* (though to Wordsworth his poems stood closer to prose than his predecessors', he understood the risk). Meter and rhyme exact their gifts from the imagination; they demand invention by necessity (the invention may be unimaginably dull, but that's another matter). Free verse requires far greater responsibility in the poet because it is our slack-jawed everyday medium—the poet must work with the currency of common speech without allowing it to *be* common. He must walk the crumbling edge of the precipice, like Gloucester—even if the precipice is imaginary. Poets who collect their lines, their lives, in free verse must resist the illusion that the mere pliancy of speech—the reflexive speech of imagination, the syntax or diction into which lines "naturally" fall—confers grace or baptizes it with interest. You can't pick up a literary quarterly without noting how often free verse submits to conventions more hobbling than meter. Why else would so many poets use the same voice, concern, attack, or sentiment?

That sounds like a brief for form.

If all poets wrote in meter, I'd be as scathing about the conventions of the iamb, the illusion that form alone gives arrest to language. I can read only so much unvaried pentameter, tedious as a minor god, without wanting to be strangled with piano wire. Free verse and form have variant attitudes and deviant intelligences; and there's no good reason why a poet should not claim one or the other according to subject, mood, whimsy, or the phases of the moon. Surely a poet should master the techniques available.

So you believe in the weight of tradition?

Our reliance on tradition is so much a matter of faith we forget we are the product of tradition. We stand on the shoulders of Lowell and Bishop, who stood on the shoulders of Auden, who stood on the shoulders of Pound and Eliot; and we ignore (perhaps we creatively misremember) what our taste for poetry, our taste *in* poetry, owes to them. Breathing their atmosphere is like tasting the lotus—we forget what we are. This wouldn't matter if the pure inhalations of tradition were progressive; but a tradition that feeds only on itself, that contains no disruptive or contrary elements, is varicose and decadent—a tradition of cannibals. Bishop and Lowell wrote in antagonism to Auden, who wrote in antagonism to Pound and Eliot. If we become little masters of American verse, content in confessional narrative or ornamental lyric, we are no longer Odysseus. We are Circe's pigs.

Which critics of modern poetry do you look back to?

Pound for his provocation, his rage of reference, and Eliot for his intuitive and submissive understanding of the art. Eliot's mole-like intimacy with the mental process of composition was unsurpassed. No other poet this century suffered such self-consciousness, but perhaps there was artistic cost. All those games of Patience, trying to grope his way back to mental nothingness. For the intelligence intimate in style, and beyond style, R. P. Blackmur and Randall Jarrell. Blackmur was a terrible poet, as terrible as only a great critic can sometimes be (we've had so many critics who were great poets, it's good to remember those who were not). I was pleased to rescue from a shelf of battered and otherwise worthless books in a Washington bookshop, only last fall, a copy of *From Jordan's Delight,* signed to a friend with his characteristic "R." It's not clear, from his haggard and mannered later criticism, whether Blackmur in the end escaped the fierce autodidact who never finished high school; but his criticism and Empson's come as close to the depths of philosophy as criticism dares. In Blackmur you have a reader of heart-stopping sensitivity, his language responsive as the language of literature—a language through the looking glass. Jarrell was our Byron, all nervous speed and verve, with little beneath the speed and verve except the most finely calibrated taste since Pound's. We were lucky to have both forms of wit, Blackmur's all gravity and Jarrell's all energy.

What about contemporary critics?

Geoffrey Hill's criticism is a month of cold baths. His austerity makes Blackmur seem first-year Latin (though Blackmur knew about delight). I read Hill with respect, because he takes the responsibility of criticism so seriously. We knew each other slightly at Cambridge in the early eighties. I remember our encounter in front of the university library one freezing morning, a few minutes before it opened. Up on the steps was a cluster of dons, and significantly Geoffrey was down in the grav-eled drive, among the students. He turned to me and said, "Up there by the door is the intellectual elite of Cambridge—Holloway, Steiner . . ." "Why aren't you up there?" I asked. "Well," he said gravely, "an educated minority might place me up there but force majeure keeps me down here." "What about noblesse oblige?" I asked, trying to make him laugh. "Noblesse oblige would have me up there," he said gloomily, "but force majeure is always stronger than noblesse oblige." He has a repu-tation for being unemotive, but he could be lively company—I once saw him imitate a hedgehog. By the time I came to write about him, in two long essays a few years later, we were no longer speaking.

I've known Christopher Ricks since my early months in Cam-bridge, and Auden was right that he's "the kind of critic every poet dreams of finding." He's like a Greek trireme at the Battle of Salamis, darting among the slower ships (and what practice and seamanship that must have required). His attention to Mil-ton and Keats has proposed, in ways only half respected in our age of theory, that the perception of language is a physical sense, almost a tactility—he is our heir to Empson.

I came to know George Steiner, the third in this triumvirate of modern critics, only a few years ago. We fell into conversation at a lawn party, and within weeks were vicious competitors over the chessboard—we favor sharp and sometimes disastrous at-tacks. Our usual defenses are the Ruy Lopez and the Nimzo-Indian. I'd been reading his essays since college, chagrined by that quality so lacking in my own, that regard for the morality of art in an immoral world. Like Pound he finds literature in the difference between cultures: he reminds us how tenuous our borders are. These critics, known by chance but read with dark affection, have affected my practice in ways deeper than I can say.

Why have you collected your early criticism?

For the discipline of being forced to. I began as a critic by reviewing novels, and thought there might be a little collection on contemporary fiction. When I read the old reviews I found I'd said nothing of interest, despite having been given some of the best books of the period. In the pieces on poetry, there was a change about 1980. Most of the reviews thereafter, and almost none before, drew something responsive from my imagination. This might in kindness be called a maturity, but if so I was a slow learner. *All the Rage* includes the raw matter, the early blind reflex of criticism, after I felt it to *be* criticism, as well as a few later reviews neglected in the design of *Reputations of the Tongue*. I have left behind reviews where the imaginative tremor was not evident. I was not a natural critic and have often resisted criticism—I wrote short reviews for nearly a decade before trying anything sustained. I look in awe at Jarrell, born breathing criticism in a style of immediate wit and sympathy—as well as a witty lack of sympathy.

But is criticism a form of morality?

Criticism is a form of attention, at best a sublime form; so it's a matter ethical as well as moral when a critic quotes, as the first two lines of "Prufrock,"

> Let us go, then, you and I,
> While the evening is spread out upon the sky . . . *

That's a comma and two words gone wrong in two lines. Of course we all make mistakes, often foolish mistakes; but a critic can't be deaf to the matter of concern. Christopher Ricks once wrote a wildly funny essay about critical error in the *London Review of Books*. When it was reprinted in an anthology, the typesetters corrected some of the mistakes he'd been at pains to criticize. An errata slip had to be issued bringing back into error the errors the typesetters had tried—again, a minor matter of ethics—to set right.

Shouldn't critics review only books they feel passion for?

A critic doesn't always choose his books. At first I reviewed whatever a distant editor sent, the good and ugly in turn; later, when I usually chose for myself, my working rule was not to

---

*Helen Vendler, *Soul Says* (Harvard, 1995), 4.

return a book simply because reading it gave me a headache. I've never asked for a book to do it harm, but I don't want the option after reading of avoiding what it would be more gracious or more politic to be silent about. The critic's duty is to give a close impression of the act of reading, its furies as well as its gratifications. Most critics love to share an enthusiasm, and I'm no different; but the critic's responsibility, the king's shilling he accepts, is to the reader—what reader wants the critic to temper his words to the author's feelings?

It's no use saying if you ignore bad books they go away—they take years to go away. Meanwhile they drive out quiet but disturbing books; and it's hard to make room for quiet books unless a critic can explain why the loud ones are haggard and empty. Most poetry reviews are exercises in genial praise, the minor publicity that attends the thin issue of thinner books. We could dismiss this as sharp practice—part of a corruption of literary value, part of a millennium-end collapse of Western culture—if it were not something worse: the intrusion of lying into an art that depends on its lies being true.

Poets say you shouldn't write negative reviews for three reasons: it's bad for poetry, it's bad for poets, and it's bad for the critic. But poetry is brawny enough to sustain criticism as severe as we expect in film or the theater; we can't erect a cyclone fence and make poetry a wildlife preserve. No one likes to receive bad reviews; but what sort of poets would we be, fed only a diet of praise, if we never even risked the critical check to our pride? Do we want readers twenty years off, or two hundred, to think we believed all our poets minor geniuses? Poetry is a dialogue, with our contemporaries and with the past; it's no good toadying to ourselves, because the past won't toady to us and neither will the future. (The future will be harsher than we can ever be—it will ignore us.) Whether criticism cripples the character of the critic or bears some small cost in regard or trivial honors is not of interest.

Critics like Jarrell enrich us with their enthusiasms. But in order to have the Jarrell who writes on Frost and Lowell and Bishop with such delight, you have to have the Jarrell who hates with passion, who can't abide sloppy work. We honor the art by being passionate toward it. Passions face both ways.

Isn't American poetry in a good period?

I wish in honesty I could say so. Most American poetry now consists of tract housing: the personal narrative is a trim backyard, a little swimming pool for the household Narcissus, and no second story. No poetry can long survive without history, without ideas, without a hidden psyche. Our best poets write as if they understood the myth of Marsyas and the cost of art: they don't need to pretend to be flaying themselves alive. I accept that, blinded in the present, we may not see one or two poets the future could honor beyond our comprehension. But the generation of Pound and Eliot and Frost and Stevens and Moore was greater than the generation of Auden and Lowell and Bishop, which was in turn greater than the generation of Hecht and Ashbery and Ginsberg and Merrill, which is a generation greater than ours. My peers should be making the dead nervous, but that isn't the case. American poetry does not depend on American examples only. To live when Heaney and Hecht and Hill are writing, when poets like Justice have found the mastery of a late style, when we have had the riches of Clampitt and look forward to the mature work of Fenton and Schnackenberg—that is not a period when a critic can fall asleep. In time this may seem a half-century of minor art, but not without major exceptions.

Notes

The Prejudice of Aesthetics

when a poet, in the broadest sense: William Carlos Williams, "The Poem as a Field of Action," in *Selected Essays of William Carlos Williams* (Random House, 1954), 288.

I'm not that conscious: "And See If the Voice Will Enter You: An Interview with Philip Levine," *Ohio Review* 16, no. 2 (Winter 1975): 48.

For some of us: Mark Strand, "Notes on the Craft of Poetry," in *Claims for Poetry,* ed. Donald Hall (Michigan, 1982), 453.

I don't want to know: Margaret Atwood, "Poetic Process?" in *A Field Guide to Contemporary Poetry and Poetics,* ed. Stuart Friebert and David Young (Longman, 1980), 25.

I just know: John Ashbery, "The Art of Poetry XXXIII," *Paris Review* 90 (Winter 1983): 53.

I am not conscious: Letters of Wallace Stevens, ed. Holly Stevens (Alfred A. Knopf, 1966), 813.

Only poets are really interested: Letters of Wallace Stevens, 491.

FORM IS NEVER MORE THAN: Charles Olson, "Projective Verse," in *Selected Writings of Charles Olson,* ed. Robert Creeley (New Directions, 1966), 16.

I would be kidding myself: Strand, "Notes on the Craft," 453.

It's best to write: David Ignatow, "The Biggest Bomb," in Hall, *Claims for Poetry,* 192.

Poetry must sing or speak: Gary Snyder, "Poetry and the Primitive," in *Earth House Hold* (New Directions, 1969), 118.

It is similar: Williams, "Poem as Field," 286.

The closed, contained quality: Denise Levertov, "On the Function of the Line," in Hall, *Claims for Poetry,* 265.

It is no accident: Reg Saner, "Noble Numbers: Two in One," *Ohio Review* 28 (1982): 7.

But I do feel: Levertov, "Function of the Line," 265.

The distinction between form: Robert Bly, "Form That Is Neither in Nor Out," in *Of Solitude and Silence,* ed. Richard Jones and Kate Daniels (Beacon Press, 1981), 24.

Ask the fact: Ralph Waldo Emerson, "Poetry and Imagination," in *The Complete Works of Ralph Waldo Emerson* (Houghton Mifflin, 1903–4), 8:54.

The form is mechanic: Samuel Taylor Coleridge, *Coleridge's Shakespearean Criticism,* ed. T. M. Raysor (Harvard, 1930), 1:224. Coleridge is following A. W. Schlegel.

[Iambic pentameter] somehow seems: Ashbery, "Art of Poetry," 54.

In an attempt to write: "Capturing the World as It Is: An Interview with Louis Simpson," *Ohio Review* 14, no. 3 (Spring 1973): 44.

I can say that we distrust: "A Conversation with Mark Strand," *Ohio Review* 13, no. 2 (Winter 1972): 58.

Romanticism's pathos of self-attention: Christopher Ricks, "Like Something Almost Being Said," in *Larkin at Sixty,* ed. Anthony Thwaite (Faber and Faber, 1982), 121.

After a period of getting away: T. S. Eliot, "The Art of Poetry I," *Paris Review* 21 (Spring–Summer 1959): 66–67.

I think the artist should master: Ezra Pound, "A Retrospect," in *Literary Essays of Ezra Pound,* ed. T. S. Eliot (New Directions, 1954), 9.

Auden's Images

1. The two liveliest and intransigently witty articles on Auden's imagery are Randall Jarrell's "Changes of Attitude and Rhetoric in Auden's Poetry" (1941) and "Freud to Paul: The Stages of Auden's Ideology" (1945), reprinted posthumously in *The Third Book of Criticism* (Farrar, Straus and Giroux, 1969). Some critics consider these essays hostile; but they are fond, even over-fond, of their subject. The form of my essay was largely proposed by Jarrell's; and the reader is urged to turn to them for a view that encompasses imagery, rhetoric, and ideology, at least until the early forties. Very early there was a late Auden. I have also taken advantage of Monroe Spears, *The Poetry of W. H. Auden: The Disenchanted Island* (Oxford, 1963), John Fuller, *A Reader's Guide to W. H. Auden* (Farrar, Straus and Giroux, 1970), and Edward Mendelson, *Early Auden* (Viking, 1981). With the exception of a remark on two revisions, all early texts have been taken from *The English Auden* (Random House, 1977) and later poems from *Collected Poems* (Random House, 1976), both edited by Mendelson.

2. Christopher Isherwood: "If I didn't like a poem, he threw it away and wrote another. If I liked one line, he would keep it and work it into a new poem. In this way, whole poems were constructed which were simply anthologies of my favourite lines, entirely regardless of grammar or sense. This is the simple explanation of much of Auden's celebrated obscurity" ("Some Notes on Auden's Early Poetry," *New Verse* 26–27 [November 1937]: 6). Edward Mendelson disputes this recollection (*Early Auden,* 147n), arguing that there were no such poems. The account is important, however, not as an explanation of obscurity, but as evidence of Auden's wicked facility, noticed also by Richard Eberhart: "[H]e'd show you a new poem and if you didn't like a line he'd strike it right out. 'Why, yes,

I see that exactly,' and he'd take it right out and he'd actually mark through it." Also, "He was writing his early poems and would change a line on the instant if you suggested it and what you suggested seemed better" (Eberhart, *Of Poetry and Poets* [University of Illinois Press, 1979], 286, 203).

3. Auden loved to reduce his knowledge to order. A number of his lists, charts, and formal organizations survive in *The Dyer's Hand* (Random House, 1962), and others in Fuller (*Reader's Guide*, 56), Spears (*Poetry of Auden*, 247) and Mendelson (*Early Auden*, 41, 68, 76, 145–46).

4. Narcissus is de-narcissus-ized by the word itself—who can grow vain without his proper name?

5. "Hugh Weston" was Isherwood's pseudonym for Auden. The whole passage is symptomatic: "Man's got to assert himself against Nature, all the *time*. . . . Of course, I've absolutely no use for colour. Only form. The only really exciting things are volumes and *shapes*. . . . Poetry's got to be made up of images of form. I hate sunsets and flowers. And I loathe the *sea*. The sea is formless" (*Lions and Shadows* [New Directions, 1947], 189). One may be wary of taking Isherwood literally. His use of pseudonyms and his prefatory admonition that his characters are caricatures may conceal either the greater or lesser accuracy of the portraits.

6. "A waiter coupled sadly with a crow," Auden wrote in *For the Time Being*. The poem would have been different, but scarcely affected, if he had written, "A banker coupled madly with a wren," "A beggar coupled badly with a gull," or "A doctor coupled gladly with a goose."

7. "Hugh Weston" was attracted to contrived vocabulary even at Oxford: "He peppered his work liberally with such terms as 'eutectic,' 'sigmoid curve,' 'Arch-Monad,' 'ligature,' 'gastropod'; seeking thereby to produce what he himself described as a 'clinical' effect" (Isherwood, *Lions and Shadows*, 191).

8. Isherwood: "The saga-world is a schoolboy world, with its feuds, its practical jokes, its dark threats conveyed in puns and riddles and understatements: 'I think this day will end unluckily for some; but chiefly for those who least expect harm.' I once remarked to Auden that the atmosphere of *Gisli the Outlaw* very much reminded me of our schooldays. He was pleased with the idea: and, soon after this, he produced his first play: *Paid on Both Sides*, in which the two worlds are so inextricably confused that it is impossible to say whether the characters are really epic heroes or only members of a school O.T.C." ("Some Notes," *New Verse* 26–27 [November 1937]: 5–6). This passage is quoted by Spears (*Poetry*

of Auden, 14), but confused with a similar passage from Isherwood's *Lions and Shadows.*

9. Isherwood again: "The scenery of Auden's early poetry is, almost invariably, mountainous. As a boy, he visited Westmorland, the Peak District of Derbyshire, and Wales. For urban scenery, he preferred the industrial Midlands; particularly in districts where an industry is decaying. His romantic travel-wish was always towards the North. He could never understand how anybody could long for the sun, the blue sky, the palm-trees of the South. His favourite weather was autumnal; high wind and driving rain. He loved industrial ruins, a disused factory or an abandoned mill: a ruined abbey would leave him quite cold. He has always had a special feeling for caves and mines" ("Some Notes," *New Verse* 26–27 [November 1937]: 8).
10. Isherwood, *Lions and Shadows,* 194.
11. Jarrell, *The Third Book of Criticism,* 144–45.
12. Auden, *A Certain World* (Viking, 1970), 424.

Books under Review

"Language against Fear"

James Tate, *Viper Jazz* (Wesleyan, 1976)

Constance Urdang, *The Picnic in the Cemetery* (George Braziller, 1975)

Leonard Nathan, *Returning Your Call* (Princeton, 1975)

Robert Hayden, *Angle of Ascent* (Liveright, 1975)

Derek Walcott, *Sea Grapes* (Farrar, Straus and Giroux, 1976)

"Two Countries"

Robert Penn Warren, *Being Here: Poetry 1977–1980* (Random House, 1980)

Seamus Heaney, *Poems: 1965–1975* (Farrar, Straus and Giroux, 1980)

———, *Preoccupations: Selected Prose, 1968–1978* (Farrar, Straus and Giroux, 1980)

"Overseas and Under"

Derek Walcott, *The Star-Apple Kingdom* (Farrar, Straus and Giroux, 1979)

Geoffrey Hill, *Tenebrae* (Houghton Mifflin, 1979)

Philip Levine, *7 Years from Somewhere* (Atheneum, 1979)

———, *Ashes: Poems New and Old* (Atheneum, 1979)

"The Present Bought on the Terms of the Past"

Donald Justice, *Selected Poems* (Atheneum, 1979)

"Younger Poets"

Marilyn Hacker, *Taking Notice* (Alfred A. Knopf, 1980)

James McMichael, *Four Good Things* (Houghton Mifflin, 1980)

Alfred Corn, *The Various Light* (Viking, 1980)

"In the Extreme"

Sharon Olds, *Satan Says* (University of Pittsburgh, 1980)

Katha Pollitt, *Antarctic Traveller* (Alfred A. Knopf, 1982)

Jorie Graham, *Hybrids of Plants and of Ghosts* (Princeton, 1980)

"The Eclipse of Style"

Galway Kinnell, *Mortal Acts, Mortal Words* (Houghton Mifflin, 1980)

Marge Piercy, *The Moon Is Always Female* (Alfred A. Knopf, 1980)

A. R. Ammons, *A Coast of Trees* (W. W. Norton, 1981)

John Ashbery, *Shadow Train* (Viking, 1981)

"Sleeping Forms"
 W. S. Merwin, *Finding the Islands* (North Point, 1982)
 James Dickey, *Puella* (Doubleday, 1982)
 Hayden Carruth, *The Sleeping Beauty* (Harper and Row, 1982)
 Karol Wojtyla, *Collected Poems* (Random House, 1982)

"Chronicle of the Early Eighties"
 Edward Hirsch, *For the Sleepwalkers* (Alfred A. Knopf, 1981)
 Leslie Scalapino, *Considering how exaggerated music is* (North Point, 1982)
 David Wojahn, *Icehouse Lights* (Yale, 1982)
 Gjertrud Schnackenberg, *Portraits and Elegies* (David R. Godine, 1982)
 Carolyn Forché, *The Country Between Us* (Harper and Row, 1981)
 Sandra McPherson, *Patron Happiness* (Ecco, 1983)
 Jon Anderson, *The Milky Way: Poems 1967–1982* (Ecco, 1983)
 Jorie Graham, *Erosion* (Princeton, 1983)
 Amy Clampitt, *The Kingfisher* (Alfred A. Knopf, 1983)

"In Exile"
 Derek Walcott, *Midsummer* (Farrar, Straus and Giroux, 1984)
 Seamus Heaney, *Sweeney Astray* (Farrar, Straus and Giroux, 1984)
 Ted Hughes, *River* (Harper and Row, 1983)
 Philip Levine, *Selected Poems* (Atheneum, 1984)

"In the Medieval Future"
 Frederick Turner, *The New World* (Princeton, 1985)

"In the Architecture of Absence"
 Vicki Hearne, *In the Absence of Horses* (Princeton, 1983)
 Mary Jo Salter, *Henry Purcell in Japan* (Alfred A. Knopf, 1985)

"Chronicle of the Mideighties"
 Louise Glück, *The Triumph of Achilles* (Ecco, 1985)
 Brad Leithauser, *Cats of the Temple* (Alfred A. Knopf, 1986)
 Richard Kenney, *Orrery* (Atheneum, 1985)
 Linda Gregg, *Alma* (Random House, 1985)
 Howard Moss, *New Selected Poems* (Atheneum, 1985)

"On Forms of Feeling"
 John Hollander, *Harp Lake* (Alfred A. Knopf, 1988)
 Rachel Hadas, *Slow Transparency* (Wesleyan, 1983)

"The Old Campaigner"
 William Meredith, *Partial Accounts: New and Selected Poems* (Alfred A. Knopf, 1987)

"Old Masters"
>   Seamus Heaney, *Station Island* (Farrar, Straus and Giroux, 1985)
>   Gjertrud Schnackenberg, *The Lamplit Answer* (Farrar, Straus and Giroux, 1985)
>   Amy Clampitt, *Archaic Figure* (Alfred A. Knopf, 1987)
>   Richard Wilbur, *New and Collected Poems* (Harcourt Brace Jovanovich, 1988)

Acknowledgments

Note: The dates in parentheses indicate the year of composition.

"The Prejudice of Aesthetics" (1984): Previously unpublished.

"Language against Fear" (1976): Originally appeared in *Poetry*, July 1977.

"Two Countries" (1980): Review of Robert Penn Warren's *Being Here: Poetry 1977–80* originally appeared in the *Washington Star*. Review of Seamus Heaney's *Poems: 1965–1975* originally appeared in the *Chicago Tribune*. © Copyrighted, Chicago Tribune Company. All rights reserved. Used with permission.

"Overseas and Under" (1979): Originally appeared in the *Chicago Tribune*. © Copyrighted, Chicago Tribune Company. All rights reserved. Used with permission.

"The Present Bought on the Terms of the Past" (1980): Originally appeared in *Crazyhorse* 20.

"Younger Poets" (1980): Originally appeared in the *Chicago Tribune*. © Copyrighted, Chicago Tribune Company. All rights reserved. Used with permission.

"In the Extreme" (1982): Originally appeared as "First Books, Fellow Travelers" in *Parnassus: Poetry in Review* 11, no. 1 (spring–summer 1983).

"The Eclipse of Style" (1980, 1981): Originally appeared in the *Chicago Tribune*. © Copyrighted, Chicago Tribune Company. All rights reserved. Used with permission.

"Sleeping Forms" (1982): Originally appeared in the *Chicago Tribune*. © Copyrighted, Chicago Tribune Company. All rights reserved. Used with permission.

"Chronicle of the Early Eighties" (1982, 1983): Review of Edward Hirsch's *For the Sleepwalkers* is previously unpublished. Other reviews originally appeared in the *Times Literary Supplement*, June 10, 1983.

"Auden's Images" (1984): Originally appeared in *W. H. Auden: The Far Interior*, ed. Alan Bold (Barnes & Noble Books, 1985). Reprinted with permission.